SEARCHING
FOR LOST LOVE

Eternal truths of   *the Lord's Prayer*

RICARDO
BENTANCUR

 **Pacific Press®**
Publishing Association

Nampa, Idaho | Oshawa, Ontario, Canada
www.pacificpress.com

Cover design resources from iStockphoto.com
Inside design by Aaron Troia

The author assumes full responsibility for the accuracy of all facts and quotations as cited in this book.

You can obtain additional copies of this book by calling toll-free 1-800-765-6955 or by visiting http://www.AdventistBookCenter.com.

Library of Congress Cataloging-in-Publication Data:
Bentancur, Ricardo.
  Searching for lost love : eternal truths from the Lord's prayer / Ricardo Bentancur.
     pages cm
  ISBN 978-0-8163-5894-6 (pbk.)
  1. Lord's prayer—Criticism, interpretation, etc. 2. Bentancur, Ricardo. I. Title.
  BV230.B465 2016
  226.9'606—dc23

                              2015033372

January 2016

Contents

Foreword

I must have been about six years old when my parents made me memorize the Lord's Prayer. It is a truly beautiful prayer! The Lord Jesus Himself taught it to the disciples on that day when He delivered the Sermon on the Mount.

His closest followers still knew practically nothing about how to pray. Like almost all their countrymen, they were ensnared in the religious formalism of that culture, tainted as it was by grossly convoluted notions. They groped around in a tangle of trifling nonsense that billed itself as refined guidance from on high.

The Pharisees, proud religious men that they were, set fixed hours each day to perform their prayers. At the predetermined moment, they would ceremoniously occupy some highly visible street corner, public square, or meeting hall, and from there impressively, with loud voices, proceed with their prayers in the hearing of all lesser mortals, staging their elitist show of pretended piety. Because of that custom, Jesus insisted, "When you pray, you must not be like the hypocrites; for they love to stand and pray in the synagogues and at the street corners, that they may be seen by men. Truly, I say to you, they have received their reward" (Matthew 6:5).

In the face of this situation, Jesus explained to His disciples that true prayer is not about spouting repetitious words in a vain, showy fashion. That kind of formal performance only cheapens the living, natural connection God holds open to His humble children. Instead, He invites heart-to-heart communication. "And in praying do not heap up empty phrases as the Gentiles do; for they think that they will be heard for their many words" (verse 7).

After listening to the Master's warning, the disciples followed with a request: "Lord, teach us to pray" (Luke 11:1). With choice words ready on His lips, Jesus taught them the famous Lord's Prayer. Of course, in doing so, Jesus did not intend for His listeners to take this model prayer and simply commit it to memory without personal reflection. To twist it into some sort of magical formula for resolving life's problems was hardly what He had in mind. That would be to fall into the same ritualistic formalism as the Pharisees. And yet, with the progression of time, this has come to pass among Christians.

The masterful prayer taught by Jesus Christ began losing relevance with the passing centuries. It took on a mystique wrapped in formality. Sing-song repetition of the lines originally spoken by the Master came to suffice in vacant minds while the powerful message it embodied largely vanished from contemplation.

This is the reason I agreed to write a foreword to my friend Ricardo Bentancur's work. He dares to rescue the significance of this prayer, and he does so with extraordinary skill. Ricardo is a talented wordsmith. He takes hold of words and colorfully creates brilliant scenes for his readers while guiding the mind to lofty heights.

It is impossible not to take delight in this book. Happily, the author does not get lost in a complicated maze of theology. This is neither an exegetical commentary of the Lord's Prayer nor an interpretation. What we have here is a practical application of each portion of the prayer to the real-life dramas we humans face day to day. Life can be cruel and merciless; sometimes it leaves us gasping for the next breath in mortal hopelessness. Looking from side to side on the horizontal plane, no way of escape appears from our pressing problems. You might be the most decided of all unbelievers, but you have nothing left except to raise your gaze to heaven and recognize your need of help.

In this book, Ricardo talks about the ravages of life. He knows from personal experience what suffering and affliction are like. This is his story. In it, he lays out some very natural human pains, such as growing up without a father at his side and other matters of everyday life, including the uncertainties all men face, the folly of bearing grudges, and the injustices of irresponsible parenting. He says, for example, that

> a child should not have to bear the hatred unleashed when parents divorce—that little one is faultless and owes them no "pound of flesh." When he becomes an adult, that will be his time to bear account for the impact his actions have on the next generation. There is no "right" by which a child's innocence is taken away. That is the rising sap that allows the little one to grow with some degree of confidence in himself and in others. But such is life, and when two adults cannot agree to protect their children, the damage they inflict can be irreparable.

I am moved by the style in which Ricardo writes. He addresses theology but does so in a subtle, gentle, and sublime way. An example of this is evident where he draws personal consolation from the phrase "who art in heaven" by weaving it into a childhood experience: "On the back wall of our apartment, overlooking the shared courtyard, someone had installed iron steps leading up to the roof deck. When things got bad for me 'down on earth,' I would climb up there to take refuge under that space of open sky. I would spend hours on the rooftop deck looking at the sky. On sunny afternoons, my gaze would follow the passing clouds as they seemed to make their way through a predetermined course, and especially on summer nights, I would climb up there to gaze at the starry sky." This simple yet beautiful way to describe divine shelter by drawing on earthly figures is the outstanding virtue of this little work.

The night I wrote this foreword, I was in Lima, the Peruvian capital, delivering a series of televised evangelistic meetings. At a little past midnight, while absorbed in reading the manuscript, the hotel reception desk rang my room to let me know that a visitor was asking for me. As it turned out, he was an old friend from my high school days. Life had taken some sad turns for him, I soon found out. His wife no longer loved him and was asking for a divorce. That cold, foggy night he had left his house to walk the silent streets in anguish. After a while, he remembered hearing that I was in town; perhaps he could look me up and unburden his forlorn despair on a friendly ear. From a corner café, he placed a number of calls until he located the right hotel. Now he was seated in my room, pleading for advice. "I've counseled a lot of distraught people over the years," he said, "but at this point in my own life, I don't know what to do."

This fellow was the epitome of pain and human impotence. What do you do when, after thirty-six years of marriage, your home life comes tumbling down like a sand castle? You ask yourself how and in what way you failed; you load on self-blame; you rationalize; and no matter how hard you search for answers in your vague memories, you draw a blank. It makes you want to wail and moan; you feel dazed as you stumble down the inner corridors of your being. The man who stood before me was living this nightmare. There are times when words offer no help. The best you can do to ease this kind of pain is to simply listen. And that's what I did. At hand on the table, my computer screen was still lit; after a while of listening, I felt an urge to read out loud a few lines from Ricardo's book.

As I read, my childhood friend rose and came over to the table to take in the written words that I was sharing. His teary, bloodshot eyes struggled at first, but he continued along with me.

Together we intoned this thought: "Faith . . . doesn't pretend to explain everything. Sometimes life events are inexplicable. Faith is not the spare tire of reason that we use when logic has deflated. How can we ever explain the death of a young child? Who is prepared to die at the age of twenty or thirty? Nobody should reasonably die at that age. We grope for reasons to alleviate our uncertainties: a terminal disease, an accident, the carelessness of a drunk driver. But reasoning falls short. The question remains: Why did God allow this to happen?"

My friend felt that his marriage had floundered, but reading that paragraph seemed to open a window where light began to enter and to dispel the shadows and relieve his pain. He wiped away an unabashed tear, looked me in the eye, and said, "Thanks."

Then, obviously comforted, he asked, "Is that from a new book you're writing?"

I said No; it was from the manuscript of another writer.

He wanted to know the author's name.

"Ricardo Bentancur," I replied.

"I don't know who he is. Where can I get a copy?"

At that moment, I realized this book would be of great benefit to the reader. It's a book that stirs the heart and answers the concerns of the soul. It carries you along on the author's life journey; sometimes you will let out a chuckle, other times it will bring tears to your eyes. There is much soul consolation in its pages, filled with hope and peace drawn from Jesus, who mastered raging storms and still does so. It leads you step by step on the journey of faith. It speaks of a God who is attentive to the pains of His children. It is a fact that in the face of life's adversities, your disciplined mind will strive to trust, but your treacherous heart will lead you to doubt. You want to believe, but the bitter experiences of life jab you so cruelly that you teeter on the edge of unbelief.

What Ricardo offers for moments like those is a healing balm. He writes,

> The heavenly Father gives meaning and direction to your steps in this world. . . . And even though you don't have a clear vision of Him, or you've wandered away from His ways, He will not stop searching for you so that you can have an encounter with Him. In time you will look back and come to see how the once-scattered dots of your life have become connected to form a picture that makes sense. . . .
>
> And behind the scenes of your own existence, where events occur of which you are not even aware, God is there at work, designing a future for you. . . .
>
> The heavenly Father possesses the key that guards the secrets of your life. He opens and closes in accordance to whether you accept His request to live in you.

The author does not confine his consideration simply to the pangs of moral suffering; instead, he turns his attention to the senseless incoherencies of human souls who, burdened by sensations of guilt, only compound their anguish through self-castigations. These souls hopelessly continue to charge their sufferings to an unburdened load of personal sins. Ricardo writes, "This is what my mother-in-law felt in her final hours. She didn't suffer so much from physical causes as she did from the notion that God was sending her suffering because of her past sins. 'I asked God's forgiveness for all the bad things I did, but now I continue to suffer.' It was not easy to get that idea out of her dear old head. The idea too readily morphs from the proposition *man sins, then suffers,* to *man sins, therefore he suffers.*"

When speaking of hatred and resentment, Ricardo does not resort to poetic euphemisms stating the obvious—that grudges, like acid, can destroy the soul, or that the heart must produce crystal-clear water to quench the thirst of others. Instead, he cuts straight to the bone:

> Sometimes resentment emerges from disappointed or betrayed love. Other times it is stirred up by envy, cowardice, feelings of humiliation, or of nonconformity with oneself, among other things. . . .
> . . . Resentment is a trap devised by disgrace.

I confess that the Lord's Prayer hardly held so much meaning for me as it does now. Every sentence, every expression, every counsel presented by Christ in His prayer opens an expanding universe of ideas that relate to our day-to-day existence. Surely it was for my soul's benefit that God put it into Ricardo's mind to ask me to write this foreword.

I would like to conclude by drawing on the story of Ricardo's birth as he movingly tells it:

> In apartment 2 on Peter Campbell Street lived a midwife named Margarita, to whom my mother turned in the wee hours one fall morning when it was time to give birth to me. Alone and bearing her intense pain, with no time to rush to the hospital, all Mother could do was pound on the adjacent wall and shout for someone to come right over to help her. Margarita answered the call, and at 3:00 A.M. a cry was heard that echoed down the hallway in that old building on Campbell Street. Mother said that I let out a wail of surprise when I arrived. And life has never failed to surprise me since then.

The truth is that if anyone never ceases to surprise me, that would be Ricardo. This book is one of those beautiful surprises. I am fully convinced that many readers will find healing from life's afflictions while their eyes glide over these wonderful lines.

Enjoy this book!

Alejandro Bullón

Introduction

How does a book come about? Why is it written? Can anyone truly say? It is like life itself. Sometimes a book appears about as unexpectedly as a youth's first love experience, suddenly jolting one out of the simpler games of childhood. Or, on the other hand, it could be planned, thought out, and hoped for like the arrival of an anticipated child ushered into the awaiting world. This book was, from all appearances, born spontaneously, motivated by an impacting happenstance. Still, its origin springs from a deep-felt clamor arising from the heart of humankind.

On a summer afternoon in 2014 here in these northern latitudes—winter in my native hemisphere—I happened upon a short two-paragraph item written by Uruguayan Eduardo Galeano. (It is with his reflection that I launch into chapter 1.) That brief anecdote tore right into my heart. The related cry of a little child from Managua hit me full force. So in effect, this work became a kind of response to that child whose prayer is the cry of a great many others. We are all in need of a father's care. This applies both to the natural order and to the supernatural one—both psychologically and spiritually.

And what better than the Lord's Prayer in response to the need you and I feel for parental care! We all long for God's love as well as for the affections of earthly arms. Out of that realization this book came about, blending together the overarching provisions of the Lord's Prayer with the underlying cravings of our humanity. This is not a theological or philosophical treatise, however. Though derived from biblical bones, it nevertheless is fleshed out with contemporary accounts. "The show," like faith itself, "must go on." Every believer lives in the awareness of universal judgment. There are the accused, there is a Judge, and there is a defense Lawyer. In this sense, Theology and Law are brothers.

Each of the nine chapters contains stories, reflections, and poetry, where the longing for God overlays the search for an absent father. That search for an absent father necessitates an encounter with the heavenly Father. With this as its central axis, the book becomes an exposition of the cardinal doctrines of Christianity, which reveals the will and life of a heavenly Father who loves us.

The Lord's Prayer is for everyone, just as the rain and sunshine, or storms and droughts, come to all. There are light and dark days in the human experience, yet the Father is never at a loss, for He knows all things. And from Him come wonderful gifts for our enjoyment in good times and allows not-so-enjoyable experiences from which to learn in times of trial. Yes, sunny days are for us to enjoy, and dark days are for us to learn from. We don't learn from pleasure but rather from pain. We can take heart in that whatever comes our way, it is already known to the Lord and never escapes His sight.

This book follows the sequence of Jesus' prayer. It flows accordingly, guided by those measured words. The Lord's Prayer follows the form of God's law, which expresses the essence of His character: *love*. God is love. From that perspective, Jesus thought out His prayer. His thinking was structured on the law of love.

Just as the Decalogue is divided into two parts, so also is the Lord's Prayer. It expresses the vertical (God-ward) upward reach of the human soul as well as the horizontal (neighborly) outreach on our earthly plane.

The first series of petitions carries us heavenward in dedication to and for Him: Your name, Your kingdom, Your will! Love finds its origin in Him whom we love "because he first loved us" (1 John 4:19). These supplications would be heard again from the cross of Calvary, pointing forward to the ultimate fulfillment of the plan of salvation (1 Corinthians 15:28).

The last four petitions offer our wretchedness to His grace: "Deep calls unto deep at the noise of Your waterfalls" (Psalm 42:7, NKJV). These are the offerings of our hope drawing upon us the eyes of the Father of mercies. It is my deepest desire that this book will be a word of life to your heart. The whole book concerns you. We all stand in need of the heavenly Father.

Chapter 1

Our Father Who Art in Heaven

The Search
Lord, I weary of life,
My throat grows hoarse
trying to shout above the waves,
the howling sea deafens me.
Lord, this life tires me so,
and the universe drowns me.
Lord, you left me alone,
all alone in this lonely sea.
Or you and I are playing
hide and seek, Lord,
or the voice with which I call
is really your voice.
Everywhere I look for you
but never seem to find you,
yet on all sides I encounter you
just for having gone a-searching.
—Antonio Machado (Spanish poet, 1875–1939)

Fernando Silva is the director of the children's hospital in Managua, Nicaragua. On Christmas Eve, he was working late. Fireworks were already going off in the streets, lighting up the night sky. He was anxious to head home, where family celebrations awaited him. One more quick pass through the wards and he would be on his way. That's when he sensed that someone was following along behind him. They were soft, padded steps, barely audible to the ear. Turning around, Fernando saw that it was one of the child patients, one who was all alone. He recognized the little boy's face, touched as it was by the pallor of an incurable disease. Those beseeching eyes seemed almost apologetic, seeking permission to

13

come closer. Fernando stood still, allowing the boy to come up to him, brush his hand, and murmur, "Tell . . . tell someone, I'm here."[1]

The loneliness of this child who was overcome by illness and suffering the pangs of a not-too-distant demise illustrates the sorrowful reality of every soul on our condemned world in this dark corner of the universe. This is the unfolding drama of the human race.[2] The cry of that child from Managua is the cry of all humanity. It is your plea and mine: "Tell someone we're here."[3]

The child from Managua reveals a fundamental human need: we are all in need of paternal care. This applies to the natural order as well as to the supernatural one; it is true psychologically just as it is spiritually.

The father figure is vital in the story of every man and woman. The ability to resolve conflicts springs largely from a child's relationship with his or her parents, and this plays a huge role in determining life's destiny. The father is not merely the one who gives us life, he is the one who protects us and gives us a sense of security. Parenting is not merely a biological act; it is fundamentally affective. Many men have children but are not truly parents. It is a fact that when the man who transmits life disappears, it becomes imperative to one's heart to replace him with some other adult who can pass on human values. An absent father produces in his child a fatherless emptiness. He or she grows up with a constant feeling of vulnerability and defenselessness. The child feels somehow responsible and guilty for causing the father to leave; thus, childhood and youth are spent struggling to be good enough to regain the acceptance and love of the father who deserted the child. Subsequently, this mechanism is transferred on to other relationships, and life becomes all the more an uphill battle. Yet where one fatherless child is unable to cope, another manages to forge ahead.

My father left home when I was five years old. I can truthfully say that my childhood was, to a large degree, consumed by the search for a paternal role model, for an adult who could operate with the force of law. I remember discussing this with my mother when I was a child. A couple of times I suggested to her men who seemed to be attractive and nice. I wanted to convince her to remarry, that she might bring home someone good, because we needed that. But she never did remarry.

In my fatherless state, our neighborhood became like a family to me, the place closest to my affections. Far from uncles and cousins, those neighbors became my loved ones. Their homes were where I spent most of my childhood hours. My neighborhood is at the source of my deepest feelings. It was my world and my place of support on earth. The community that surrounds a child, together with the family, is the originating horizon where the threads begin to intertwine to set the course for life's unfolding story. And there, very close to me in that neighborhood, was the seed of Christian faith that germinated in my mother and, in turn, would mark my destiny.

Across the street lived Dr. Landoni, a physician with a silver mane of hair, an elegant man with a serene gaze. His wife, a plump and charming woman, dedicated herself completely to her family. They had two children, a boy and a girl who was my age. Watching her leave each morning for school was like an awakening for me. Her blond hair, which fell to her waist; her gentle blue eyes; and her gazellelike steps stirred in me a rush of inner energy, the zest of the beginning of a crush. But she was an unreachable princess.

The next-door neighbor to the left of our apartment was a man by the name of Demarco, an Italian man whose wife, when he wasn't seen for a period of time at his usual haunts, would say he was "on vacation." Although the other neighbors said he was in jail.

A couple of houses farther down Peter Campbell Street, there was a cheap hotel where two prostitutes, Betty and Gloria, lived. They were sort of a stigma in that middle-class neighborhood. Betty's and Gloria's sons were my buddies, Enrique and Bobby, who in our playful Hispanic way, we nicknamed "Bobo" (which would be like calling someone a dimwit or a goof in English). Both of them were good and supportive friends.

Farther up the street, near Rivera Avenue, lived the Bojorge family. Their son William to this day is still my friend. His dad was the director of the British School. William played rugby with the Old Boys team at the British School; they were the classic adversaries of another team called Old Christian. It was this latter team, as you may recall, that was featured in the famous *Alive: The Story of the Andes Survivors*. On October 13, 1972, the Uruguayan military plane carrying them to Santiago, Chile, crashed high up in the mountains. Only sixteen of those boys, out of all the passengers and crew, survived. They were rescued on December 23 of that same year. What a miraculous Christmas gift that was for those families, especially for the renowned painter Carlos Páez Vilaró, who never abandoned hope during the search for his son. After more than two months, the press presumed them all dead, but not so for Páez Vilaró. I still remember that father's face the day he embraced his rescued son.

Right next to our apartment there was a popular sports center called Campbell Street Bowling. In the back of that establishment, there was a small apartment with walls adjacent to ours. It was a kind of hideout where delinquents could flee to avoid being captured by the police. The night before he was shot, a notorious criminal named Mincho Martincorena went into hiding there. His assaults caused serious havoc in Montevideo. The neighbors came up with a ditty after his demise: "Martincorena, unfit to live, died riddled like a sieve."

Right in front of our apartment lived Amanda, the piano teacher. I don't know if she was truly ugly or if my frustration with learning to play that instrument made me see her that way. Memories can sometimes be apocryphal. But she was a good person with infinite patience. I spent the most torturous hours of my childhood during those unwelcome classes. I hated those classes, which my mother paid for from the small housecleaning salary she earned. My mother always said that education was the only way out of poverty, which, ever since my father had left us, seemed as if it had taken up residence with us on a no-eviction basis. My mother bought us books with much hard work and sacrifice, telling us that a child who reads becomes an adult who thinks.

My memory takes me to apartment 2, adjoining ours, with which we shared a common hallway that led to an open-air courtyard, which was sixteen feet long by thirteen feet wide. It was like a dirt square with brick walls ten feet high that separated our unit from the neighbors'. There was one lone pine tree in that space; I watched its growth over time, always elegant, reaching up toward the sun. Nature always offers an encouraging message of hope. There was also enough space for my mother to raise a few chickens, whose eggs added a bit to our household finances. I will hold off telling you for now about the family who lived in apartment 2. First, I want to focus on something else.

"Who art in heaven"

On the back wall of our apartment, overlooking the shared courtyard, someone had installed iron steps leading up to the roof deck. When things got bad for me "down on earth," I would climb up there to take refuge under that space of open sky. I would spend hours on the rooftop deck looking at the sky. On sunny afternoons, my gaze would follow the passing clouds as they seemed to make their way through a predetermined course, and especially on summer nights, I would climb up there to gaze at the starry sky.

The earth is our unique habitat in the universe. It is our foothold and place of support. Everything that moves on this planet has the earth as a point of reference: just as a river flows according to the lay of the land, giving it a channel and direction, we can make all our movements thanks to the firmness and the support of the ground beneath our feet. In addition, the land we occupy is nourishing. The Creator determined that from the earth would come our sustenance (Genesis 3:17), and to it we return at death, because "you are dust, and to dust you shall return" (verse 19).

But sometimes the earth beneath our feet behaves strangely: it moves beneath our feet, provoking a certain degree of terror. This is true both literally and metaphorically. Earthquakes occur not only in physical geography but in the human geography as well. Suddenly, we realize that the ground on which we tread is not as firm as we believed it to be.

On those days when the earth "moved" underneath my feet, I would turn to the heavens and climb up to heaven, that place that is never shaken or moved. The earth would move beneath my feet when the "war of the sexes" intensified, meaning the heated conflicts between my mother and father. And that overarching heaven offered me a great escape.

Heaven is the earth's ultimate foundation: in its remoteness and infinite distance, it envelops us, and its fixed stars guide us toward the glory of the Creator. Just as the stars guided the Magi from the East on their way to Bethlehem, heaven also guides you when you get lost on earth. This is true in the natural order of things as well as in the spiritual. The heavens provide us with a map. On the days of anguish, the rooftop deck of our apartment was my calm refuge. In those moments, the earth was nothing more than a fleeting ship that moved through space, and the heavens above an infinite place of security.

The Bible declares that "the heavens are telling the glory of God; and the firmament proclaims his handiwork" (Psalm 19:1). The immense depth of a star-studded night reveals the infinitude in which our world seems to be lost. In their profoundness, the heavens pull us out of the confines of our limited human existence, while at the same time allowing us to loosen the bonds of life's anxiety in order to perceive the footprint of the Eternal. When the anxieties and worries of your daily existence feel like they have a stranglehold on you, keep calm, look up, and contemplate the starry heavens. You will return to your everyday world renewed.

At the same time, there is another essential characteristic of heaven: from it emanates time as a dimension in which our past, present, and future occur. While the earth is where all our daily activities take place, heaven determines when these things take place. To heaven belong the day and the night, light and darkness, and the course of the seasons and years. Immense galactic spiraling accompanied by innumerable solar cycling demarcates for pensive creatures the course of time. Our day and night, light and darkness, seasons and years, are all the interplay of earth with the far beyond. The earth's rotation on its axis determines the daily rhythm, and the planetary revolutions around the sun determine the annual cycle. In this way, the astral heavens mark the time of our personal existence, while signaling the finitude of our mortal condition.

The heaven of heavens

But the heavenly Father is far beyond and yet closer than the heavens that I could see from my rooftop. "Our" heaven was created during the first week of

Creation (Genesis 1). The Genesis account of the Creation week did not include the heaven where God has dwelt from eternity:

> The LORD is in his holy temple,
>> the LORD's throne is in heaven;
>> his eyes behold, his eyelids test, the children of men (Psalm 11:4).

It was this "third heaven" that the apostle Paul referred to when he wrote, "I know a man in Christ who fourteen years ago was caught up to the third heaven—whether in the body or out of the body I do not know, God knows" (2 Corinthians 12:2).

Referring to the Creator, the psalmist writes,

> to him who rides in the heavens, the ancient heavens;
>> lo, he sends forth his voice, his mighty voice (Psalm 68:33).

"Whatever the LORD pleases he does, in heaven and on earth" (Psalm 135:6) because to God, there is no difference between heaven and earth. Nothing can contain Him. He exists beyond all creation and beyond space and time, but He enters with sovereignty into our history.

The search for a Father

We said that the boy from Managua poses the great human need: we are all in need of a father's watch care. This is true both in the natural order as in the supernatural.

I do not think that the absence of my earthly father was the *cause* behind my search for a heavenly Father, but it was the *condition* that opened the way for my encounter with the Lord. *Cause* and *condition* are not interchangeable terms. What causes water to boil is the fire; the boiling condition of the water is all about the pot in which the water boils. The initial circumstances of my life were what set me on a course for an eventual encounter with God.

Doesn't it sometimes happen that when you walk down memory lane you see flashbacks like paintings on a wall more or less in an ordered sequence? It almost seems like someone placed them that way intentionally. Could it be that there is a superior Intelligence that is made known in the grandeur of nature and in the way certain circumstances have come about in your life?

In apartment 2 on Peter Campbell Street lived a midwife named Margarita, to whom my mother turned in the wee hours one fall morning when it was time to give birth to me. Alone and bearing her intense pain, with no time to rush to the hospital, all Mother could do was pound on the adjacent wall and shout for someone to come right over to help her. Margarita answered the call, and at 3:00 A.M. a cry was heard that echoed down the hallway in that old building on Campbell Street. Mother said that I let out a wail of surprise when I arrived. And life has never failed to surprise me since then.

Margarita had a husband, who was an army captain; he was a frugal man of few words but known for his generous heart. My brother promptly nicknamed him Papa Flores. That family practically became my brother's second home. By God's gracious design, Papa Flores filled the role of surrogate father to my brother during most of his childhood. Pocho and Mima, Papa Flores's children, became like a brother and sister to him.

But the best of what God had in mind for us came from Margarita, the wife and mother of that family. She was a believer and a woman of simple, practical faith. She had a strong sense of service combined with a great love for others. This was not so much expressed in words as in actions. Margarita became a wonderful friend to my mother and planted in her the gospel seed, which in time would germinate within her heart.

A heavenly Father

When we elevate our hearts to God, we do not direct ourselves to "something," we do not immerse ourselves in some cosmic energy, as Eastern philosophy postulates; neither do we fuse with the "mysterious totality of the universe." We are addressing "Someone," a person. Because the God of the universe is a personal Being who wants to relate with us face to face, He is attentive to the desires and needs of our hearts. Prayer directs us toward that Being who is our beginning and end. The Lord's Prayer begins with an invocation and ends with exaltation to the same Father: the Alpha and the Omega. The beginning and the end of everything. Saint Augustine, in his *Confessions,* wrote, "You have formed us for Yourself, and our hearts are restless till they find rest in You."[4] When we say the word *Father,* we direct our whole being toward the only One who loves us, understands us, and forgives us, because we are His children. In Him, we find the beginning and the end of our lives. In the Lord's Prayer, Jesus uses the Aramaic term *Abba,* a close and intimate way of referring to the Father. It means "Dad" or "Daddy." The word *Father* can sometimes arouse a certain type of fear. But *Abba* is a personal and close Being.

"Our Father who art in heaven" points to the ultimate foundation of this earth, to Someone who is beyond the vicissitudes of the world. It expresses the fact that beyond the happenings of your life there is an infinite God who is not subject to time or sickness or decrepitude and death. He is your mighty fortress and your refuge in time of trial. You can say with the psalmist,

> The LORD is my rock, and my fortress, and my deliverer,
>   my God, my rock, in whom I take refuge (Psalm 18:2).

The heavenly Father gives meaning and direction to your steps in this world. The Lord says,

> I will instruct you and teach you
>   the way you should go;
>   I will counsel you with my eye upon you (Psalm 32:8).

And even though you don't have a clear vision of Him or you've wandered away from His ways, He will not stop searching for you so that you can have an encounter with Him. In time, you will look back and come to see how the once-scattered dots of your life have become connected to form a picture that makes sense.

Behind the ebb and flow of world events, the rise and fall of empires and nations, there is a God who controls the universe. We have nothing to fear, because

> "He changes times and seasons;
>   he removes kings and sets up kings;
> he gives wisdom to the wise
>   and knowledge to those who have understanding" (Daniel 2:21).

And behind the scenes of your own existence, where events occur of which you are not even aware, God is there at work, designing a future for you:

> Yet it was I who taught E'phraim to walk,
>   I took them up in my arms;
>   but they did not know that I healed them.
> I led them with cords of compassion,
>   with the bands of love (Hosea 11:3, 4).

The heavenly Father possesses the key that guards the secrets of your life. He opens and closes in accordance to whether you accept His request to live in you.

> Every human tie may perish,
> Friend to friend unfaithful prove,

Mothers cease their own to cherish,
Heaven and earth at last remove;
But no changes
Can attend Jehovah's love.

—Thomas Kelly

FOR YOUR REFLECTION

1. What does the expression "Our Father who art in heaven" mean to you?

2. Can the absence of an earthly father serve as the *condition* that leads one to seek the heavenly Father?

3. What is Jesus Christ's Father like? Describe Him in your own words.

4. Who are we addressing when we elevate a prayer to God?

---

1. Eduardo Galeano, *El libro de los abrazos*.

2. For the believer, life is a drama and not a tragedy. In a drama, the character roles can be altered; while in a tragedy, the characters are predetermined by fate. For that reason, a drama always finds resolution, while a tragedy does not. In tragedies, the key characters always die. The difference between these genres of literature and theater is seen in how the closing scenes play out. Dramas work toward solutions in life, while tragedies do not.

3. It was brought to my attention that the human interest story concerning the little child from Managua left some readers wondering about his cry and whether there was ever a comforting response to ease his loneliness and give him the emotional support and love he needed as he faced his closing scenes. I realize that it may seem to some that my incorporating just a snippet from that child's life—the most emotionally impacting moment of his suffering existence—was, to a degree, philosophically or theologically exploitative. Some readers, I am sure, needed follow-up on that little fellow's "rest of the story." You and I can connect via the thoughts expressed in this book, and we may do so in the warm comfort of our respective homes, but it would be tragic to lose perspective about the very real suffering of many innocent children and people of all ages in far less pleasant circumstances than we enjoy. It is not just a lonely Christmas Eve for a dying boy in a sterile hospital ward; there are millions of hungry people, war-displaced orphans, and hopeless persons crying out for care, kindness, and the warmth of affection that lasts beyond a fleeting moment in this literary presentation. God knows how the life of that little child in Managua unfolded; He knows as well the far better story prepared for him in the Promised Land. We may not have the possibility of discovering more concerning that particular precious one's closing scenes on earth, or even his name, but God is ready to open before us similar stories where we can each be the answer to a personal cry, one that will not be lost in the great impersonal mass of misfortune.

4. Saint Augustine, *The Confessions,* 1.1.

Chapter 2

Hallowed Be Thy Name

If I Adore You
Oh my Lord,
If I adore you
for fear of hell,
scorch me in its fire.
If I adore you
for the hope of paradise,
impede my access to its door.
But if I adore you
only for yourself, grant me then
the beauty of your face.
—Rabi'a al-Adawiyya (Muslim female poet, 717–801)

There are at least two things that arouse in us amazement in this world: the beauty and harmony we see on earth and the majesty of the heavens. We enjoy beauty; the greatness of the heavens inspires in us awe. Nothing impacts the human soul quite like the sensation of mystery hidden in a star-studded night. The spirit of man is sensitive to the elusive yet real message of nature. This notion is so universally held that we conclude that a person must not be fully human if he cannot perceive in the beauty of earth and the majesty of heaven, even vaguely, the sublime presence of God.

Here and there, we are surrounded by mystery and wonder. Flowers, in their efforts to survive, demonstrate the same traits as animals: they hunt to feed, and they show themselves off to reproduce. They attract bees, bugs, and beetles to carry their pollen, and they pay for that service with nectar and pollen. They entice not only insects but also animals, such as bats, birds, and possums, to do their will. In service to the flowers, hummingbirds lend their needlelike beaks, bumblebees buzz, and opossums offer their tongues. Some plants are carnivores, while others, like the honeysuckle, entice with their sweet aromas. It is such a grand symphony.

But is not this harmony proof of the existence of an infinite and provident Intelligence? Yes, but the footprints of God in nature are not enough for us to get to know the Eternal One. So why do we subject ourselves to the disquieting provocations of Someone who seems beyond our ability to know—One who might even cause us fear and resignation? The answer is clear: we are simply unwilling to submit to loneliness. Our cry is like the cry of the child from Managua: tell someone that we are here! Deep within our hearts, we cherish the conviction that Somebody must be out there watching over us. We need that care. Not only do we need to know that there is a God, but we need to feel Him close beside us. We need to know that He sees us and that He loves us.

Common sense tells us that creatures are not born with impulses and desires unless there is the possibility of satisfying those impulses and fulfilling those desires. If we are hungry, there is something called food. If a duck desires to swim, there is water. If a bird has the urge to fly, it flaps its wings and takes to the sky. "If I find in myself a desire which no experience in this world can satisfy, the most probable explanation is that I was made for another world."[1]

Where are You, God?

When my mother got angry, my brother and I were treated to hearing the wisest sayings from the language of Cervantes, such as, "The water pitcher makes so many trips to the brook that it finally breaks." When she said the word *breaks,* we knew her patience had reached its limit and it was time to flee to the rooftop deck. Sometimes my mother had to fill the man's role and enforce the law in our home. It was not easy for her to be both mother and father. We climbed like cats up those iron rungs leading to the rooftop, and from the skylight encompassing the communal courtyard, we would watch her movements. When the "storm" finally passed, we would go back down to the flat to take comfort in restored peace.

But the roof deck was not only a place of refuge, it was also a laboratory for intergalactic fantasies. From there, I sailed up into the clouds and navigated from horizon to horizon. Especially at night, the majesty of heaven inspired me with awe. Although these reflections that follow arose with conceptual clarity in my adult years, my childhood heart already sensed that there must be an Intelligence that created all that I could see spread before my upturned gaze and everything around me. I longed to know that Being who exists "beyond the stars."

But what possible good could it do me to ponder the existence of a superior Being to better my chances in this world? To grasp the existence of a Creator expressed in the majesty of the heavens seemed to me to serve no social or biological purpose. It didn't make any useful sense for the development of my life on this planet. We human beings are quite limited after all: it is next to impossible to transmit to others our personal experiences with the sublime or incorporate that perception with scientific knowledge and much less with practical life. For this reason, the great English scientist Stephen Hawking declared himself an atheist. He looks at nature but fails to see any sign of an infinite intelligence behind it.

Something more is needed

When I moved to the United States, I felt like a certain French neighbor when she first came to live in my boyhood neighborhood. Learning a different language is such a frustration. Let me share with you my confusion with the English language from a few of my poetry verses below:

> *English . . . so foreign*
> *to my ears.*
> *It wasn't Shakespeare*
> *but Cervantes*
> *who determined*
> *my destiny.*

> *Flee these sounds;*
> *into exile retreat.*
> *My Castilian tongue*
> *safe shelter seeks,*
> *as a bloodied soldier*
> *in confused defeat.*

> *I haven't a clue*
> *what a* book *is*
> *or a* star
> *or this metallic guttural sound that translates into a* kiss.

> *One knows full well*
> *that it is the lips*
> *that carry the weight.*

> *However, noticing my suffering,*
> *You drew close to me to tell me*

something that I understood as if
spoken to me in my native Castilian tongue

Cuando las palabras callen
Mi corazón
Te hablará
En silencio.

(When words fail,
My heart
will speak to you
in silence.)

The need to communicate is essential for a human being. The last verse offers hope: When words fail, My heart will speak to you in silence. The heart always seeks a way to communicate even without words.

In the house next door to the Landoni family, a French family had arrived from Paris "fleeing from civilization" (Europe still was suffering the consequences of the Second World War). That family consisted of an elderly woman (to my child's eye, a graying head could mean anywhere from thirty-nine to seventy-nine years of age), a daughter in her thirties, and a dog. They knew very little Spanish. But the smile on the aristocratic face of the "elderly French woman" (as we called her at home) made communication easier. I remember the struggling effort she made to utter the simplest of phrases, such as, "Hello . . . good morning, Ricardo." Her near paralysis in trying to speak Spanish produced a kind of emotional spasm in me. I wanted to speak for her. Maybe that's why we became friends. So, a couple of times each week, I crossed the street, with its old-style pavers, to "teach" her Spanish. In return, she taught me French.

In her home, I came to know of Maurice Chevalier, and I learned my first words in the language of Baudelaire. Wishing to communicate and being a great reader, this well-educated French woman learned the Spanish language quickly. Even though her pronunciation of certain words, admittedly, left my ears red with embarrassment. Soon she could give information and even communicate ideas and feelings. One dark afternoon late in October 1967, I saw the French woman's daughter crying over the news that Che Guevara had been killed in Bolivia. In my neighborhood, many young people joined the ranks of the Tupamaros, a leftist revolutionary movement; it was the first urban guerrilla movement in Latin America.

The need and ability to communicate isn't the exclusive legacy of human beings.

In some measure, animals are also able to express themselves and communicate. But what sets us humans apart is not just the ability to express ourselves in words and symbols but that we feel an obligation to draw a distinction between the *expressible* and the *inexpressible*. Only the human creature experiences awareness that things exist beyond our ability to express in words. What is most astonishing by far is not what we understand and are able to communicate but what is within reach and yet escapes our comprehension. The effort to convey what we sense by intuition but cannot put into words is the everlasting theme of humanity's unfinished symphony. We sense that there is a God. "If God did not exist, it would be necessary to invent him," François-Marie Arouet, better known as Voltaire, said.[2] But we do not possess the power to reach the highest peak of intellect and from that vantage point neatly conceptualize God, nor do we have wings that allow us to soar beyond all our human imperfection. Allow me to paraphrase the German philosopher Immanuel Kant, who expressed the foolish illogic of reason in its attempt to reach the Eternal: the bird that cleaves the air, and feels its resistance, might conclude it could fly better in a vacuum.[3] Human reason can only "fly" in the atmosphere of earth. We cannot reach beyond our senses.

For that reason, there is practically nothing we can say about God based on data collected from the surrounding world. Yet we see glimpses of the existence of God in every feature of human history and nature. Sunshine, timely rain, snowy hills, and crystal rivers declare the love of the Creator. We perceive evidence of God's attributes in the relations of filial and fraternal love: the shared affection among family members, spouses, parents, and children:

> As a father pities his children,
>   so the LORD pities those who fear him (Psalm 103:13).

However, the same sun that testifies to the loving Creator can turn the earth into a scorched desert, provoking drought and famine. Torrential rains and mud can inundate entire villages. Those majestic mountains we admire can belch lava, boulders, and ash, burying entire population centers. And what shall we say about human relations? They can deteriorate into jealousy, envy, anger, and hatred, culminating in murder. Clearly, the revelations about God gleaned from the natural world too often confuse us and leave us in deep anguish. So what sense can we make of our existence if in the end we simply die, not knowing whether there is anything more for us out there beyond the stars?

Wise Solomon says,

> What does man gain by all the toil

at which he toils under the sun?
A generation goes, and a generation comes. . . .
There is no remembrance of former things,
    nor will there be any remembrance
of later things yet to happen
    among those who come after (Ecclesiastes 1:3, 4, 11).

Everything is forgotten. Do you doubt this? Just try to remember the given and family names of your great-grandparents. Were you able to? If you can, try next to recall your great-great-grandparents' names!

The gentleman of faith and the gentleman of resignation

There are two possibilities open to man in the face of his awareness of mortality. That, at least, is the way Danish philosopher Søren Kierkegaard saw it. Let me relate in condensed version a story he once told.

Once, a humble village lad felt strangely perturbed. Something was happening to him that he couldn't control. He unexpectedly lost his sense of reason, and his heart seemed possessed of an absurd passion: he had fallen head over heels in love with a beautiful, delicate princess. Everyone could see as plain as day that this love had about as much possibility of succeeding as a tender seed planted in a salt flat. All of his good and wise friends, as well as his own common sense, told him to give up his wild fantasy and instead turn his attention to what was possible and to set his sights on what was realistically obtainable: there was a certain widow of a rich beer brewer, and though she was a bit uncouth and not very good looking, lacking in natural grace, she still would be a good catch for the likes of him.

But, like a sliver in his flesh, those thoughts and passions for the princess persisted and grew ever stronger. The passing of time only seemed to fan more intensely the flame of his love. Finally, abandoning all common sense, the young man threw himself fully into the arms of the absurd. At that point, he said to himself, "By faith alone, faith in my absurd love, I'll change from being merely a peasant villager and instead become a gentleman. I'll make of my existence a living testimony of chivalry and my bearing will surpass that of any prince. My faith will soar higher than reason, high above the simple possibilities this world offers the likes of someone like me. By virtue of my absurd faith, I will win the hand of my princess."

Kierkegaard uses the figure of the young peasant to refer to the believer struggling with his faith in a world that only offers vain pleasures to distract the anguish of humankind. The world has no answer to the tragedy of death, just nothingness. For Kierkegaard, the princess represents immortality, eternal life won by the valiant in the quest for the kingdom of heaven. Jesus said, "From the days of John the Baptist until now, the kingdom of heaven has been forcefully advancing, and forceful men lay hold of it" (Matthew 11:12, NIV).

But there is another character that appears in Kierkegaard's tale: the gentleman of resignation. He represents atheists and false believers who only try to understand the world by human logic and cold calculation. They do what seems most convenient to their interests. They never dream.

By their reckoning, they are the sane ones. The believers are the "crazy" ones, according to the description given by the apostle Paul: "The unspiritual man does not receive the gifts of the Spirit of God, for they are folly to him, and he is not able to understand them because they are spiritually discerned" (1 Corinthians 2:14). The gentleman of resignation believes it most realistic to squelch any desire for the princess and to immerse himself in resignation to numb the pain. This gentleman is a gentleman in the lowercase form. He becomes numb in the everyday things; he tries to fill his void by consuming things that are inconsequential; and this in turn consumes him entirely. He lives only for today and for the present world. His motto might well be "If the dead are not raised, 'Let us eat and drink, for tomorrow we die' " (1 Corinthians 15:32). The gentleman of resignation cannot sacrifice his daily interests for the deeper passion of achieving the impossible. Residual unhappiness is repressed by the pretense of how good things seem to be going in his material world. But deep within, there is nagging uncertainty. Every night when he lies down next to the widow, he is hounded by a pestering thought: *And yet, it would've been so much better to have won the hand of the princess.*

Only the gentleman of faith is genuinely content. His reigns over the finite because his faith rises over his possibilities. The gentleman of faith is fully convinced that with God nothing is impossible. He is courageous because the world has not imposed on him a widow. He will die fighting and suffering for his faith, but in that battle there is hope and dignity.

The search for God

What is less probable than overcoming death? Apparently nothing! Eternity and personal salvation are shown again and again to be absolutely impossible in our human condition. The evidence of all observable life seems to say exactly that. Look, for example, at the advancing decrepitude of your parents. They once were young, but now observe how they have aged. More and more of our dear elderly folks have gone to their silent rest, their voices no longer heard. Reason tells us as much: a tree lives longer than a human. The universe remains but an individual passes. Logic tells us that the laws of physics are necessary and immutable. But for argument's sake, let's accept that the universe is irrational and there somehow exists a thing called an immortal soul. Take a sincere look within you and around you: do you or anyone of us really deserve salvation? We are a miserable lot, full of selfishness. How many times have we collaborated with our little grain of sand in the vast work of injustice and death! We couldn't possibly sacrifice what's in our wallets or give offerings and tithes, and yet we require the universe to sacrifice its laws so that we can be saved! We are truly lost. But, fortunately, what is impossible for man is possible for God. "But Jesus looked at them and said to them, 'With men this is impossible; but with God all things are possible' " (Matthew 19:26).

Kierkegaard says, "Just because I see no way out, I must never have the audacity to say that therefore there is none for God. For it is despair and blasphemy to confuse one's own little crumb of imagination and the like with the possibilities God has at his disposal."[4] When you find yourself in a pit of uncertainty, try to remember that the situation at that moment is not your final destination; the best is yet to come. Do not despair nor find refuge in pride, because your future is in God's hands.

The Bible: the source of truth

Unless God revealed Himself to man, humanity would never have come to know Him. The cry of humanity would never have received an answer. Because God is holy, humans can only know Him by the revelation He makes of Himself in His Word. *Holy* means "separate, self-sufficient." Holiness, omnipresence, and omnipotence are attributes exclusive to God. His sinless perfection or purity is the essence of His "otherness"—His transcendence. So unless He took the initiative to reveal Himself to us, we could never have known Him, much less have hoped for something better than this world.

The human being who does not conform to the things of this world and seeks the Eternal is found by the Eternal. The thirst for God that overwhelms us is an echo of the thirst that consumes the heart of God for our souls:

> My heart says of you, "Seek his face!"
> Your face, Lord, I will seek (Psalm 27:8, NIV).

Human memory is fragile, but God's memory is eternal:

> Your name, O Lord, endures forever,
> your renown, O Lord, throughout all ages (Psalm 135:13, NRSV).

But the LORD sits enthroned for ever (Psalm 9:7).

He remembers you and me, all our ancestors, and those who are to come over the centuries. Our life is hidden in Him.

> But let all who take refuge in you be glad;
>> let them ever sing for joy.
> Spread your protection over them,
>> that those who love your name may rejoice in you (Psalm 5:11, NIV).

We are not alone in the universe, because the Holy God of Israel comes to us and communicates with us through His Word.

Through the Word of God we know that there is a Creator:

> By the word of the LORD the heavens were made,
>> and all their host by the breath of his mouth. . . .
> For he spoke, and it came to be;
>> he commanded, and it stood forth (Psalm 33:6, 9).

And only through the Word of God can we know that He has a purpose for our lives:

> Thus says God, the LORD,
>> who created the heavens and stretched them out,
>> who spread forth the earth and what comes from it,
> who gives breath to the people upon it
>> and spirit to those who walk in it:
> "I am the LORD, I have called you in righteousness,
>> I have taken you by the hand and kept you;
> I have given you as a covenant to the people,
>> a light to the nations" (Isaiah 42:5, 6).

The Bible is the greatest revelation of God. Its sixty-six books, it can be said, are sixty-six volumes of a single masterpiece whose parts are harmoniously inter-related. The Holy Bible is God's letter to humanity written with the blood of the prophets on the scroll of time: over a period of fifteen hundred years, authors of the widest diversity—from peasants to kings, from poets to prophets—penned God's dream for humanity. The central theme of the Bible is the Father's love: "For God so loved the world that he gave his only Son, that whoever believes in him should not perish but have eternal life" (John 3:16).

When my mother became a Christian, she began reading the Bible with urgency, as if wanting to recover lost time. The God she found in those pages was a great God. She used to read me some portions of the Bible before going to bed. She would read to me short stories and some inspiring psalms. My mother loved the Psalms. Some of the more cumbersome texts would put me to sleep quickly, but others were so captivating that they kept me wide awake. And it wasn't lacking in chapters of bellicose literature that gave way to incredibly frightening nightmares. (I am not a fan of this kind of literary genre for children.) Some scenes from the Old Testament are the ancient version of the bitter ongoing wars between Jews and Arabs today; the dust of millennia has not yet been able to bury all that cruelty.

When I think back to what it was that attracted me to the Bible during my childhood years, I would say with certain clarity that it was two values: the authenticity of the Bible and the message of hope. The characters in the Bible were people of flesh and bone. Authentic. Good and bad. Real. They were as varied and contradictory as people walking the earth today. Now that I am older, that same sensation of authenticity is still a convincing reason for my attachment to the Bible. The transparency of God's Word is what credits it with lasting value. In addition to the profession of truth, what impacted my young life even more was that it brought peace to my young heart with its message of hope:

> listen to the LORD who created you.
> . . . the one who formed you says,
> "Do not be afraid. . . .
> I have called you by name; you are mine" (Isaiah 43:1, NLT).

> The LORD called me from the womb,
> from the body of my mother he named my name (Isaiah 49:1).

Someone was watching over me. Someone was watching over my steps. I knew that I would not walk alone in this world. Like the child from Managua, I longed for that watch care. And the Word of God satisfied that need.

A psychologist would say that was an unsatisfied need brought on by my father's abandonment when I was barely five years old. Yet with that explanation I would still feel empty. God has never let me down, even when at different stretches of the road I wasn't aware that He was right beside me, watching over me and guiding my steps.

Hallowed be thy name

Interestingly, the expression "hallowed be thy name" is the first of seven petitions found in the Lord's Prayer. It parallels what we find in the first of the Ten Commandments, which similarly calls on the faithful to sanctify and honor God's name. God comes first. And therefore, this petition is converted into a testimony of recognition of the Most High, an expression of desire to enter into a relationship with Him. Sanctification begins when the petitioner invokes God's holy name. The same name that was revealed to Moses (YHWH) and later to Jesus. So strong is this testimony that it results in an imperative for the soul:

Bless the LORD, O my soul;
and all that is within me, bless his holy name (Psalm 103:1).

To bless the name of God is to enter into His plan of salvation for humankind.

We cannot express "hallowed be thy name" if the sanctity of God is not revealed beforehand in our hearts, if we do not invoke the name of the Lord.

The Old Testament employs different names for God: *Elohim,* source of power (Genesis 1:1), *Elyon,* the Most High God (Genesis 14:18–20), *Adonai,* the almighty ruler (Isaiah 6:1). These names emphasize the majestic and transcendent character of God. Other names reveal the willingness that God has to enter into a relationship with humankind: *Shaddai* describes God as the fountain of blessings and well-being (Exodus 6:3). The name *Yahweh,* translated as "Jehovah" or "LORD," emphasizes the faithfulness and grace of God concerning the covenant with His people (Exodus 15:2, 3). In Exodus 3:14, *Yahweh* describes Himself as "I AM WHO I AM," indicating His unchanging relationship with His children. But at other times, God has provided an even more intimate self-revelation, in presenting Himself as "Father" (Deuteronomy 32:6) and in referring to Israel as "My son, My firstborn" (Exodus 4:22, NKJV; Deuteronomy 32:19).

Except for the name *Father,* the names of God that appear in the New Testament have equivalent meanings to the names in the Old Testament. In the New Testament, and more precisely in the Lord's Prayer, Jesus uses the term *Father* to bring His followers into a close and personal relationship with God (Matthew 6:9). The Father of Jesus Christ is also the Father of the divine Family.

In the Bible, there is one God, which is a unity of three coeternal Persons: the Father, the Son, and the Holy Spirit. In contrast to the surrounding pagan nations, Israel believed in the existence of only one God (Deuteronomy 4:35). The New Testament places the same emphasis on the unity of God (Mark 12:29–32; John 17:3). But this monotheistic emphasis does not contradict the Christian concept of the Trinity—the Father, Son, and Holy Spirit—rather, it affirms that no pantheon of diverse deities exists.

While the Old Testament does not explicitly teach that God is triune, it is no less certain that it refers to a plurality within the Deity. Sometimes God uses plural pronouns: "Let us make man in our image" (Genesis 1:26). In various references, a distinction between God and His Spirit is made. In the story of Creation, we read, "The Spirit of God moved upon the face of the waters" (Genesis 1:2, KJV). Some texts not only refer to the Spirit but also include a third Person in the work of man's redemption: "And now the Lord GOD [the Father] has sent me [the Son is speaking] and his Spirit [the Holy Spirit]" (Isaiah 48:16);

> Behold my servant [the Father is speaking] . . . ;
> I have put my Spirit upon him [the Son];
>   he will bring forth justice to the nations (Isaiah 42:1).

We cannot but see the Son in the Father whom Jesus invoked in prayer. Jesus' teachings about Himself provide us a much clearer vision of the triune God. In John 14:11, we read, "Believe me that I am in the Father and the Father in me." And when He revealed who He was, those who heard Him fell to the ground because they knew He was declaring Himself equal to God (John 18:6; also Exodus 3:14). The following text is explicit: "The Jews then said to him, 'You are not yet fifty years old, and have you seen Abraham?' Jesus said to them, 'Truly, truly, I say to you, before Abraham was, I am.' So they took up stones to throw at him; but Jesus hid himself, and went out of the temple" (John 8:57–59). Jesus was reminding the Pharisees that He was the "I Am" of Exodus 3:14. For that supposed blasphemy, they wanted to kill Him.

All through his Gospel, John reveals that the Godhead consists of God the Father (chapter 3), God the Son (chapter 4), and God the Holy Spirit (chapter 5), a unity of three coeternal Persons, linked by a mysterious and very special relationship.

A temple in time

The Bible does not speak of relics or holy places, as promoted by religious marketing, such as the shroud of Turin or locations in Jerusalem Jesus frequented. That said, however, there is a holy lapse of time. The fourth commandment reminds us: "Remember the Sabbath day by keeping it holy" (Exodus 20:8, NIV).

When I was ten years old, the Flores family moved out of apartment 2 on Campbell Street and the Perez Machado family moved in. The Flores family had bought a large house near the beach; and since my brother missed Papa Flores so much, he went to live with them for weeks at a time. That left only my mother and me at home. The new neighbors didn't know the Flores family, or us, for that matter. They had a nine-year-old daughter, Mabel, who was unbearable; so I didn't want to have anything to do with them. Mother, however, wanted to be a good neighbor, so she would bake cookies for them and ask me to take them over.

Every week something strange happened at the Perez Machado home that aroused our curiosity: every Friday afternoon they gave special attention to cleaning their apartment, and at dusk an aroma of fresh baked bread wafted in the air, mingled with religious melodies. My mother and I wondered what sect the Perez Machado family belonged to. There was something intriguing about those Friday afternoons, and at the same time, it was something we found pleasant. Finally, one Friday evening my mother's curiosity got the better of her and she decided to take them a plate of cookies herself while they were singing. Jose and Victoria cordially invited her in and explained that they were "receiving the Sabbath." They welcomed my mother to join them in reading the Bible and singing songs. Since that day, my mother never stopped reading her Bible. The Perez Machado family invited her to attend evangelistic meetings with them. A famous preacher named Salim Japas conducted the meetings, which were held at the Astor theater in late 1962.

One of the Bible studies my mother received during that evangelistic series was about the Sabbath, the day of rest. Accustomed to going to church now and then on Sundays, it was quite a surprise to her when she read the fourth commandment in Exodus:

> "Remember the Sabbath day by keeping it holy. Six days you shall labor and do all your work, but the seventh day is a Sabbath to the LORD your God. On it you shall not do any work, neither you, nor your son or daughter, nor your manservant or maidservant, nor your animals, nor the alien within your gates. For in six days the LORD made the heavens and the earth, the sea, and all that is in them, but he rested on the seventh day. Therefore the LORD blessed the Sabbath day and made it holy" (Exodus 20:8–11, NIV).

Victoria and Jose taught her that sanctifying God's name also includes keeping the Sabbath day holy, to seek Him in that temple of time that is the day of rest. Ever since then I remember how my mother always looked forward to the arrival of the Sabbath when she could gather together in community with the faithful and worship God. The Sabbath became a time of weekly rest for my mother, who was preoccupied with the stresses of life. But it was Jesus, the Lord of the Sabbath and Prince of Peace, who gave her heart rest. Without Christ, the Sabbath day would have just been another religious holiday, a break from the weekly routine, a day of leisure. But with Christ as its focus, it became the greatest blessing she received in her life.

FOR YOUR REFLECTION

1. Are there traces of the existence of God in nature?

2. What is the only source of truth by which to know God?

3. What comprises the Deity? Read Genesis 3:22; 1 Corinthians 8:4–6; Ephesians 4:4–6; and 1 Timothy 2:5.

4. What is the period of time each week that we must sanctify?

---

1. C. S. Lewis, *Mere Christianity,* 120.

2. *Wikiquote,* s.v. "Voltaire," last modified December 2, 2009, https://simple.wikiquote.org/wiki/Voltaire.

3. Immanuel Kant, *Critique of Pure Reason.*

4. Søren Kierkegaard, *Søren Kierkegaard's Journals and Papers,* vol. 5, 6135.

Chapter 3

Thy Kingdom Come

Andrew
The afternoon was slipping by in Palestine
When I saw the face of that Nazarene
The Grace of that good Man
Nailed in His sacred heart the sacred thorn.

"Come and see beloved brother
A Master Pilgrim
Without the boasting of the Greek
Nor the pride of the rabbi."

And in that crossroads
When the sun was lost on the far horizon
Came forth a kingdom and a destiny.

He gave confidence
To the heart of the lost
And offered a new song of praise.

—Ricardo Bentancur

The poem "Andrew" is based on John 1:40, 41: "One of the two who heard John speak, and followed him, was Andrew, Simon Peter's brother. He first found his brother Simon, and said to him, 'We have found the Messiah' (which means Christ)."

Andrew's invitation to Peter was among the first testimonies that helped inaugurate the kingdom of God on earth. The central theme of the message and life of Christ is the kingdom of God. From as far back as Old Testament times, the coming of the kingdom was already being announced: we find this in the books of the prophets, in the Psalms, and in the historical records of Samuel, Kings, and Chronicles. So the Hebrew people were well acquainted with the phrase "the kingdom of the Lord" (1 Chronicles 28:5).

The New Testament doesn't contain a different concept than the Old Testament about the kingdom of God. True, the famous parables of the kingdom appear in the Gospels (Matthew 13; Mark 4; Luke 8), but did Jesus' parables change the essence of the kingdom of God from that presented in the Hebrew Scriptures? By no means! For Christ came "to confirm [not to change] the promises made unto the fathers" (Romans 15:8, KJV).

As a good Israelite, Jesus was instructed by His parents concerning the kingdom of God; and as His faith and His relationship with His heavenly Father grew deeper, this concept became ever clearer and more profound in His mind and heart. He felt sent of heaven to announce its presence to all who would listen.

Was there, then, any originality in the message of Christ? Yes, most certainly: He was the only Jewish prophet who said, with absolute conviction, that the kingdom of God, long announced in Scripture, was not a mere promise but a reality. And further, He Himself was in charge of making it a present reality among men. Let's remember what took place at the synagogue in Nazareth:

> Jesus returned to Galilee in the power of the Spirit, and news about him spread through the whole countryside. . . .
>
> He went to Nazareth, where he had been brought up, and on the Sabbath day he went into the synagogue, as was his custom. And he stood up to read. The scroll of the prophet Isaiah was handed to him. Unrolling it, he found the place where it is written:
>
> "The Spirit of the Lord is on me,
>   because he has anointed me
>   to preach good news to the poor.
> He has sent me to proclaim freedom for the prisoners
>   and recovery of sight for the blind,
> to release the oppressed,
>   to proclaim the year of the Lord's favor."
>
> Then he rolled up the scroll, gave it back to the attendant and sat down. The eyes of everyone in the synagogue were fastened on him, and he began by saying to them, "Today this scripture is fulfilled in your hearing."
>
> All spoke well of him and were amazed at the gracious words that came from his lips (Luke 4:14–22, NIV).

In other words, wake up to the fact that "the kingdom of God is within you" (Luke 17:21, KJV).

These words spoken by Jesus caused a great impact on His audience, but only a few of those people believed in Him. It would take time, but it was necessary for the kingdom of God to display all its power during the three and a half years of Christ's ministry. And so the truth was spread gradually: God was already present, and His presence and actions started to cause wonderful things to happen in the lives of people and in the history of the world. The days of the kingdom of darkness were numbered, while the kingdom of grace was already an active reality for the good of everyone.

Jesus knew, and therefore taught, that His words and actions did not yet fully constitute the complete and glorious manifestation of the kingdom of God (which we will see in the last chapter of this book), but He showed in and through those efforts that God Himself was actively working in the world through the love of His Son. The task of those who saw and heard Him was to open their hearts to receive Him and accept Him, so that they could begin to live better lives and to live with the hope of a better future.

Jesus was not a theologian dedicated to the theoretical explanation of the doctrines of God. He came to announce the divine purpose among men. He doesn't ask us to perfectly grasp the essence of God. He simply asks for an invitation to come into our hearts: "I stand at the door and knock; if anyone hears my voice and opens the door, I will come to him and eat with him, and he with me" (Revelation 3:20).

Today Jesus asks the same of you and me. The question is, How do we go about receiving Him into our hearts so that we can enter into His kingdom?

Pleasant aromas

Memory is everything. Oblivion is death. Thanks to memories, we can bring to the present our childhood and adolescence, our youth, the summer and autumn of our existence. A simple melody can bring back emotions of bygone years. I always wonder what would have become of us without those songs that brought melody and rhythm to our daily hours. With what song or melody did you awake to life and to love?

But there is nothing more powerful for our recollection than certain aromas that impregnate our memories. It's hard to forget the scent of some perfumes. Doesn't the simple aroma of a particular food bring back certain memories for you? What types of memories come to your mind when you smell the fragrance of honeysuckle or jasmine in the spring or the pleasing aroma of damp earth after a summer rain?

When my wife and I had been married for a "sufficient" number of years, I wrote her a poem. Sometimes one needs to revisit the path taken. What better way than to sort and arrange some memories? I wandered down the halls of the past, stopping here and there to smell the fragrances. In the first stanzas, I touched on that chaotic and long-suffering succession of bittersweet smells from my childhood and adolescence: "the smell of red wine, / of cigarettes, / of polenta and thyme," up until my young adulthood, when Florencia, my wife, appeared. The verses now changed, and I must confess that in that moment:

Everything was scented of you

Of jasmine
Of freshness

I asked myself
If you were real

Your perfume
Raised a feeling
Of uncertainty

The scent of purity and innocence
The essence of you scenting the air
While entwining your power
Within my memory

Today your lovely fragrance persists

When I recited my poem to my wife, she responded skeptically, "Don't lie. I don't think I could smell the same today as I did years ago." Romantically inspired, I slipped into the kitchen and planted a kiss on her neck as she was chopping an onion. As my lips landed on the little birthmark at the beginning of her hair line, which her German grandmother liked to call "the tree of life" (*der Baum des Lebens,* reminiscent of an ancient Teutonic legend), I still sensed the aroma of the youthful years gone by. There is something eternal within mortal time that remains in a fragrance. It is said that time consumes everything but love, which remains like an imperishable aroma. All of creation moves under the influence of love because "God is love" (1 John 4:8).

As reflected midway through my poem, my life changed categorically in my youth: when I was eighteen, I came to know Jesus Christ, and at twenty, I met Florencia. Those two events marked a wonderful turnabout for me. However, the bittersweet smells did not readily leave room for the new sweet aromas. The transition from "unpleasant odors" to the "new, sweet fragrances" of life was neither seamless nor automatic. There was skepticism in my heart and a degree of uncertainty (alluded to in the poem). I struggled to understand that a new and better world could really open up for me.

Why do we put up so much resistance to receiving God's gift of grace?

Why do we humans believe that if we receive something it is because we somehow deserve it? Why do we believe that nothing is free in this world and that everything has a price? We wonder cynically: How much is this or that person worth?

The questionable values of this consumer society stick to the soul like dust to the feet of a traveler. Transactions of every sort imaginable constantly take place—sales, purchases, acquisitions—and they all depend upon money. Everything has its price, and everything demands sacrifice on our part. We must pay the price for anything we want. We must earn the right to deserve it. And this same mentality is carried over into the emotional plane as well. Marriages, of whatever type they may be, are rather contracts of goods and damages, of rights and responsibilities, of rewards and punishments, of the limits of our economic capabilities. It seems that less and less grace exists in human relationships.

But what precisely is grace if not an undeserved favor, a free gift bestowed on us? I have wondered many times why we reject grace. What is in our hearts when we reject love? Why do we settle for living so poorly? Why do we confuse love with weakness?

A couple of days ago, I spoke with a young woman who had been abandoned by her father and raised by her stepfather. Her mother treated her with cold indifference. There is a terrible destructive power in a mother's emotional disinterest. This girl had never had a boyfriend. She could not form relationships with others her own age. She would reject anyone who approached her despite their best intentions. She interpreted any kind of affection as an expression of weakness and scorned anyone who showed her love. Her latest object of anger and frustration was the woman her stepfather had recently married. This new member of the family was now her personal hell. But this young woman had one little glimmer of joy in her life: her cat. The cat was, according to her, the only one who understood her.

After talking with her for a couple of hours, trying to understand the dynamics of her emotional relationships, I asked myself what real chances were there for a person to be able to love if she hadn't learned the art of love because no one had ever loved her, had ever shown her love. What possibilities are there to love without the capability to love? What is the margin of freedom to transform her life?

This is a vital matter for the destiny of any person. This goes for you and me. The ultimate worth of a human life is determined by character, and character is defined by the ability to love and be loved. In relation to this, faith plays a crucial role. To know that God loves us makes a real difference. When we seek His love and are nourished by it, a change occurs in our character, producing a corresponding effect upon our ultimate destiny.

We resist God's grace because we don't know how to interpret it. It has become ever scarcer in the surrounding world; and there seems to be less and less reference to it among those around us. We resist divine grace because we consider it a weakness, an affront to our personal freedom. We believe we can get by on our own.

Many of us conclude that all we need to do is exercise the freedom with which we were born. Even when professing a certain religion, we don't believe in divine grace because we don't believe in the power of God for our lives here and now. Consequently, religion becomes a matter of empty rituals.

This is an old story. Centuries ago, a man named Pelagius (354–420) held the belief that every good and evil thing could be attributed only to human freedom. Grace was just God's external action that caused man to respond to the Creator by following the model of Jesus Christ. Jesus was therefore something of an exemplary model—a Mandela, a Gandhi, or a Martin Luther King Jr. But for Pelagius, there was no "internal" grace because human freedom cannot be maintained if God also acts on the interior of man to move him toward doing good.

This interpretation was strongly opposed by Augustine of Hippo (354–430), who stressed the irreparable damage of sin and the absolute necessity for divine grace in order to be able to do what is good and to live according to the commandments of God. Augustine's position followed that of the apostle Paul, who wrote,

> For I do not do the good I want, but the evil I do not want is what I do. Now if I do what I do not want, it is no longer I that do it, but sin which dwells within me.
>
> So I find it to be a law that when I want to do right, evil lies close at hand. For I delight in the law of God, in my inmost self, but I see in my members another law at war with the law of my mind and making me captive to the law of sin which dwells in my members. Wretched man that I am! Who will deliver me from this body of death? Thanks be to God through Jesus Christ our Lord! (Romans 7:19–25).

This grace that comes from Jesus is granted to us without any merit of our own; it is given freely (hence the term *gratia*). It doesn't inhibit or block personal freedom because it acts by attraction, by love. What is not moved by love cannot be moved by anything or anyone. When it reaches the heart, God's love has no remedy, but it is the cure for all of life's ills. Jesus said, "And you will know the truth, and the truth will make you free" (John 8:32). Since the time of slavery in this country's history, the story has been told of a slave who, after being purchased by a rich man and set free from his condition as a servant, decided to give himself to his new master, to whom he said, "You have made me free, so now I will serve you forever."

Grace is the only way in which God relates. Although the term *grace* finds more resonance in the New Testament, especially in the writings of Paul, nevertheless the Old Testament presents a similar concept. For example, *chen* is the Hebrew word used most frequently in reference to unmerited favor. "Now therefore, I pray, if I have found *grace* in Your sight, show me now Your way, that I may know You and that I may find *grace* in Your sight" (Exodus 33:13, NKJV; italics added). A legalistic reading of the Old Testament does not perceive the richness of the word *grace* in those writings. But grace is from ancient times and is everlasting: Ezekiel 36 and Isaiah 49 are songs about the grace of God.

The kingdom is like a misunderstood father

Among the Bible parables about the kingdom of God, the one found in Luke 15 is, in my opinion, the best one: The young man had become completely bored with his father and the rest of his family. He couldn't bear any longer the monotonous rhythm of his daily life—the same old routine day in and day out. Sunsets brought him no warm satisfaction of a day lived joyfully. His nights were nothing more than a blanket of darkness oppressing his soul. His elderly father didn't offer him any type of prospect.

Tired of seeing his father's wrinkled face and watching him hobble around, weak and worn, the young man felt that there was no future for him at his father's side. This young man, like so many others, had his vision clouded by a past that he could not regain nor one that contained any good memories. It seemed to him that his father had never been young, strong, protective, or fun. For that reason, he decided to flee the nest. In his selfishness, he didn't have the decency or the sensibility not to ask for that which did not belong to him: his inheritance ahead of time. Finally, he got up the nerve to lay out his thoughtless demand before his father. Maybe it didn't even cross his shallow mind that in effect he was writing off his elderly father as already dead. He asked for it, his father gave it to him, and he wasted it. On friends and strangers.

How many children easily forget that the elderly father who now trembles, who babbles and can barely talk, is the one who in earlier years held them in his strong arms when they were weak and defenseless, when they were just beginning to live!

Having at last fallen on bad times, reduced to eating the same slop he was hired to feed to pigs, the young man's thoughts began to turn back to the best days of his childhood and youth. And he decided to return home. He resolved that he would go home as a common laborer to eventually earn enough to repay his father what he had squandered from the inheritance. Along the way he practiced his sincere plea: "All I ask is that you give me a job as one of your laborers."

That afternoon, his father waited for him to come home like so many times before: with his arms open wide, outstretched into the distance, as infinite as his pain, as ample as his love. When the old man saw his son approaching, he closed the distance between them; he ran toward him, he embraced him, he kissed him. He didn't even let his son finish the words he had memorized during the long journey home. He commanded his servants, "Bring quickly the best robe, . . . bring the fatted calf . . . , and let us eat and make merry" (Luke 15:22, 23). Nothing could be greater for a father's heart than the return of a child, than a reencounter with that child who "was dead, and is alive again" (verse 24).

There was celebration and rejoicing at the house and in the old father's heart. It was as if everything had returned to normal. Now the father's home radiated with the light of hope and peace.

However, the eldest son "was in the field" some distance from the house (verse 25). Although he had always lived with his father, close to him physically, his soul was far away from him. He was as far away emotionally and spiritually from his father as his younger brother had been physically during all those years. Many children live their entire lives far away from their father's home, without entering it. What would happen to our soul if it were to die with the heart out "in the field," far from an encounter with the one who gave us life?

The eldest son heard music, but his cold heart persisted in distancing himself from the celebration and joy. His sense of justice was stronger than his mercy, stronger than the grace that the father had shown his younger brother. He had always worked at his father's house, he had never left, he had never squandered the inheritance, and he had always fulfilled his duties. As far as he was concerned, his father's grace was irresponsible and unjust. Therefore, "he was angry and refused to go in" (verse 28), even though "his father came out and entreated him" to join in the celebration.

The essence of grace is to rejoice with the person who receives an undeserved good. After all, who among us really deserves the good things that freely come to us? The eldest son was upset that grace was bestowed on someone with no saintly halo circling his head, no badges of heroism decorating his chest; bestowed on someone who had not left honorable footprints in his family's history and was not good news in the headlines of society. His younger brother had returned home penniless and smelling like swine, disheveled, a human skeleton, someone deserving of nothing. But this is what the message of the kingdom of God is about: grace for the wretched and disgraced.

This resonates in my own life: to accept my brother Orlando, nicknamed Pepe, for who he was. To love him. To not compete with him. I'm ashamed to admit it, but as a child I hated my brother when I would see him play soccer so well, but especially when the girls would seek him out—because women love the guys who score the goals. I don't know why. Or better said, I do know why: they love winners. But who am I kidding? Of course, I know why: they love champions. All men know this from an early age. Everything we do has the sole purpose of attracting the opposite sex and pleasing them. It's as if a female's role is none other than to be our ideal, that which will guide us and mold us as such. During the adolescent years, when everything is a foggy confusion, life is an open competition between boys to measure their skills with the purpose of becoming the favorite of a girl.

It's in the blood. It has always been the case since early European history, according to the Spanish philosopher José Ortega y Gasset, who points this out in the first canto of the *Iliad* where the woman appears as the prize awarded to the one who is the victor of the games or of war.[1] To the bravest belongs the most beautiful woman. Thus, since the origins of our history, we see man aspiring to conquer a beautiful woman. But what we fail to realize is that the woman is not just destined to be the prize given to the best man; she is in charge of judging which man is the most worthy, so she can select the most excellent one. In other words, the woman does the choosing. This killed me. Today, I realize it.

My brother was a great midfielder. He played in the youth division for Club Atlético Defensor and Club Atlético Peñarol, the latter of which was the best twentieth-century team according to FIFA (Fédération Internationale de Foot-ball Association). I once thought he could never become a professional soccer player because he didn't have a father around to guide him. It's not that he lacked talent or the courage to defend me with punches and blows on the street against whoever was bothering me. He always fulfilled his duty as my big brother; he protected me. He was stronger than I was. But I envied him, and that mental mechanism that led me to be jealous of his talents and to compete with him eventually, with time, took root in my character. And though he perhaps wasn't aware of it, my jealousy toward him was projected in my relationship with him during the years of my youth. It took many years for me to fully accept, love, admire, and respect him without the slightest shadow of envy. That came about only when my heart received divine grace.

Grace signifies that during the soccer match of our lives the referee blows his whistle, announcing the game is over. Grace declares all of us winners, even though we played the game poorly. The competition is over.

So, therefore, there is no need to struggle to behave like saints in order to win God's favor. Hypocrisy is ended. We no longer must secure our own worth by the sweat of our brow. The competitive struggle to beat others at the game of life is ended. At church we no longer need to spy on our brothers and sisters to see whether they are playing the game well. That's all over; we are no longer competitors or spies. Christ has already secured the victory for us.

The older brother of the parable needed a conversion just like that of his younger brother. The life of the older brother was not as dramatic and outwardly dishonorable as that of the prodigal; this older brother's main fault was that he believed only in himself. To have an encounter with Christ, it isn't necessary to hit rock bottom in life. Ellen White said, "Conversions are not all alike. Jesus impresses the heart, and the sinner is born again to a new life. Often souls have been drawn to Christ when there was no violent conviction, no soul rending, no remorseful terrors. They looked upon an uplifted Saviour, they lived. . . . This conversion was genuine, and the religious life was just as decided as was that of others who suffered all the agony of a violent process."[2]

From the parable of the oldest son, we learn that an individual right in which the defense depends on the rejection of mercy is in reality an abuse. The oldest son was apparently without fault, but the gospel story teaches us that faithfully performing our moral duties is not enough for us to gain acceptance from God. Rectitude alone is not enough: when it is separated from love, it can fatally blend with resentment and hatred. Instead of healing, it brings sickness. Justice can negate justice if love does not penetrate it. We can profess a faith, fulfill all the rituals of a creed, but if we have not had a personal encounter with the Father as the prodigal son did, we cannot know God. We cannot know His grace or enter His kingdom.

This parable might reflect your life or mine with its two ways of rejecting the grace of God: that of the prodigal son and that of the older brother. In this parable, we see a picture of God and a picture of each one of us; we discover that we have within us much more evil than we had thought and that God loves us much more than we can fully fathom.

But essentially this is a parable about the Father who is in heaven; largely misunderstood by humanity, His love is always far greater than any evil, and His mercy does not allow resentments. It is the Father who is at this moment knocking on the door of your heart, waiting to be invited in without any reservations.

Give thought to these words: "Lord, take my heart; for I cannot give it. It is Thy property. Keep it pure, for I cannot keep it for Thee. Save me in spite of myself, my weak, so unchristlike self. Mold me, fashion me, raise me into a pure and holy atmosphere, where the rich current of Thy love can flow through my soul."[3]

FOR YOUR REFLECTION

1. Why was Andrew's invitation to Peter important?

2. What does Romans 3:24 mean to you?

3. Why do we resist God's grace?

4. Think of three lessons from the parable of the prodigal son.

---

1. José Ortega y Gasset, *Estudios sobre el amor.*

2. Ellen G. White, *Selected Messages,* book 1, (Washington, DC: Review and Herald®, 1958–1980), 177, 178.

3. Ellen G. White, *Christ's Object Lessons* (Washington, DC: Review and Herald®, 1941), 159.

Chapter 4

Thy Will Be Done, on Earth as It Is in Heaven

Whatever You Want

Whatever You want, Lord;
let it be whatever You want.

If You want me to laugh among the roses
every morning,
the splendors of life,
let it be whatever You want.

If You want me, among the thistles,
to shed blood unto the unfathomable
shadows of eternal night,
let it be whatever You want.

I'll be grateful if You want me to see,
I'll be grateful if You want me to be blind;
I am grateful for everything and for nothing;
let it be whatever You want.

Whatever You want, Lord;
let it be whatever You want.
—Juan Ramón Jiménez (Spanish poet, 1881–1958)

Life brings its share of hard times—times of crisis—when we seek almost in desperation to know the will of God. Because we know deep within that we cannot do it alone. Because we are confused. In those moments, the psalmist also raised his voice to the Most High:

> Make me to know thy ways, O LORD;
>   teach me thy paths. . . .
> Relieve the troubles of my heart,
>   and bring me out of my distresses (Psalm 25:4, 17).

Sometimes our lives seem to be navigating in rough seas and turbulent waters. Then we turn to God just as the panicked disciples did during the storm on the Sea of Galilee: "And behold, there arose a great storm on the sea, so that the boat was being swamped by the waves; but he was asleep. And they went and woke him, saying, 'Save, Lord; we are perishing' " (Matthew 8:24, 25). They were afraid. They were confused.

My conversion to Christianity had much to do with the type of storm that is unleashed in the mind and heart when life moves past the first phase. When we begin to enter into the second decade, toward maturity, these years are times of confusion. The teen years represent for many the roughest waters to negotiate in life; at times, it feels like the boat is getting pummeled by mounting waves of confusion. Life begins to collect on the debts not paid from the emotional needs of infancy and early childhood. The errors of youth can leave permanent scars. Life has this injustice: we have to make decisions at times when we are the least experienced. What do we want to become when we grow up? Whom will we marry? Is there a God? What does He want for us? So many questions. Too much to think about for the future when we can barely live in the present, tormented by our hormones. The mind doesn't think or know, and the body is in control.

There are just too many questions for a blossoming soul to deal with. There were too many questions for my lonely heart to face. How many young people throw their lives away, without opportunities for second chances, simply because they have no family to support or guide them! We should never condemn young people for their bad decisions. They are not to blame. We adults are the ones at fault.

In my particular case, it wasn't simply about a vocational crisis but a terminal one. Every crisis is terminal. There was a crisis that I wanted to drown out with alcohol for a time. My past had come crashing down on me. It was then, one summer morning, that I returned home empty of myself, after several sleepless days and nights. I flopped on my bed and was surprised that the ceiling began to spin. I wasn't drunk. My head was burning with intense pain. I tried to sleep, but I couldn't. For two full days, I remained stiff, without eating and with my eyes wide open. I couldn't move my left arm and leg, and half of my face was paralyzed. My mother then called Dr. Landoni, the doctor who lived across the street from us. We never wanted to disturb him. He seemed to me like a saint of a man, nothing less than a great doctor. You just don't bother people of such exalted status. But my mother, in her desperation, got up the nerve to knock on his door. He hurried right over!

He touched my forehead. There is some sort of magic in the white coats doctors wear! How much of an assurance of healing power is felt in just a tender touch! I spilled out my anguish to him: "I want to die." He gently replied, "You're not going to die. You're much too young. This is happening because you have too much fire in your soul. Give life to your dreams." He prescribed me a medication. Mother told me later that I had been on the verge of having a stroke. I came out of it OK. But I learned from it.

Crises can be good. The word *crisis* comes from the Greek verb *krinein,* which means "to separate" or "to decide." The term *critic,* which derives from the word *crisis,* has this meaning of "separating" the terms of reasoning to determine whether it is correct. The word *criterion,* then, refers to proper reasoning. The Greeks gave four meanings to this same word, *crisis:* the culminating moment of an illness, a dispute, choice, and judgment. In other words, a crisis is the end of a culminating moment in life that requires us to make a choice, and it always produces a radical change. If we resolve it, we are launched toward a better future. Just like an arrow is first drawn back on the bow before shooting forward, the trials of life that seem to drag a person back might in reality be just the tension needed to launch that person forward to a better future.

"Give life to your dreams." I no longer had dreams. (Many never live out their dreams because they are too occupied living their fears or their frustrations and hatred.) However, God had a dream for me. To seek Him and know His will for my life was my second task. As soon as I set out to fulfill that task, I learned that my time on this earth could have drastically come to an end.

What is the will of God?

It's not easy for mere mortals to know what God wants from us, or what we can expect from God in one circumstance or another. Asking what God's will is seems to be a natural question. But even when we raise the question, we know that it is not reason that has the ultimate answer. You may wonder whether it is going to rain tomorrow, and the weather forecast will provide you with an informed answer. You can calculate what time you'll get home if you know how many miles you still have to go. But sometimes it is unclear whether God wills for you to leave a job, move to another city, end a relationship, or enroll in one university rather than another. Since all decisions have consequences, for this reason we want to be certain that what we do is God's will. But we don't always have a logical answer or the absolute proof that leaves us with peace of mind. There are answers to some questions that require much patience and wisdom. And some questions will, seemingly, never receive answers.

God's will for our lives is also open to misinterpretation because of our own human limitations. For example, a sick person might believe that his disease is a divine punishment. A woman might convince herself that her husband's beatings are God's will for her and she must "bear her cross" with resignation. But what if her husband continues his violence and she ends up in the hospital, or worse? It is this kind of fatalistic vision that leads us to confuse the will of God with the negative things that happen to us.

Even more so, in some circumstances, we can convert the question about what God's will is into something trivial, insubstantial, and egotistic. This happens when we confuse divine will with our own desires and petty interests. As was the case with a pious elderly lady, who while in the midst of a terrible drought, when the farmers depended on the rain for their families' livelihood, prayed: "Please don't let it rain because I don't want my new church shoes to get wet." Certain prayers are the result of an immature Christianity, selfish and superficial. God's will may not coincide with my own will:

"For my thoughts are not your thoughts,
     neither are your ways my ways, says the LORD.
For as the heavens are higher than the earth,
     so are my ways higher than your ways
     and my thoughts than your thoughts" (Isaiah 55:8, 9).

Suffering and divine will

The question regarding the will of God becomes highly relevant in the midst of suffering. For a mother who has just lost her child, this question takes on a whole different meaning. A few days ago, I received this message on my cell phone: "Pastor, you cannot know, and I hope you never have to experience it, the pain my heart feels. How can I bury my son, this child whose breath I can still feel inside me?" A relatively young woman had lost her child to cancer. What words could I offer? Silence seemed better. And then she sent me these words: "I know that my Redeemer lives." Here was a woman of faith. From this horizon, the question about the will of God is a fundamental question. Its answer rests more on a response from the soul than from the reasoning of the brain.

Faith doesn't explain the reasoning behind why things happen. It doesn't pretend to explain everything. Sometimes life events are inexplicable. Faith is not the spare tire of reason that we use when logic has deflated. How can we ever explain the death of a young child? Who is prepared to die at the age of twenty or thirty? Nobody should reasonably die at that age. We grope for reasons to alleviate our uncertainties: a terminal disease, an accident, the carelessness of a drunk driver. But reasoning falls short. The question remains: Why did God allow this to happen?

God is love

God is love. "The glory of Him, who moves all things, penetrates the universe," says Dante Alighieri in *The Divine Comedy*.[1] Love is the force that spins the stars in the universe. The heart of a mother guards the secret behind that force. And although a woman might forget the fruit of her womb, the Lord never forgets His own:

> "Can a woman forget her sucking child,
>   that she should have no compassion on the son of her womb?
> Even these may forget,
>   yet I will not forget you" (Isaiah 49:15).

God extends His arm across the abyss. The question regarding the presence of evil and suffering in the world that underlies the issue of God's will for your life and mine brought anguish to Job's life. But the patriarch received an answer in his heart because he perceived the universal vision of all things.

Job was aware that all his afflictions were side effects of a great cosmic conflict between good and evil, a conflict in which the consequences are suffered by innocent people. The same occurs in wars. But he also knew that, as an innocent victim of a cosmic conflict for which he was not responsible, he was still under the mercy of a God who does not forget His own. Therefore, in the midst of his suffering, he exclaimed:

> "For I know that my Redeemer lives,
>   and at last he will stand upon the earth;
> and after my skin has been thus destroyed,
>   then from my flesh I shall see God" (Job 19:25, 26).

Some theologians see in these words of the patriarch the prophetic announcement of the resurrection of Christ, who is the hope of all who believe in Him (John 3:16).

A few days ago, I visited the home of a friend who was recovering from ovarian cancer, a collateral effect of the great cosmic conflict. When it came time to say Goodbye to her and her family, I prayed this prayer: "Lord, in the valley of the shadow of death may we be able to see our Redeemer in the midst of the great controversy in which You are waging the war against evil." By the profound sighs and strong "amens" uttered by my friend and her daughter, I could tell that those intercessory words gave her hope and comfort. To see ourselves in the context of the story of redemption gives rest to our hearts. It is soothing to the soul to know the will of God in the midst of suffering!

The faith that sustains the one who is suffering and is upheld during those times of pain is a determination of the soul, an act of love. It is the act that opens a pathway where none previously existed. It is the force by which the soul excavates a passage between mountains of darkness to come into the light. It is the fruit of an intense and constant vigil, of a faithful persistence to a vision. This faith is not improvised, although it sometimes appears at the least expected moment, as the arm of Christ reaching down to uphold Peter in the midst of the waters of the Sea of Galilee (Matthew 14:30, 31).

True faith is the desire to keep open our channel of communication with God, and to do so in the face of the raging winds and waves, even at the cost of life itself. It is the art of trusting God, of feeling His presence in our daily lives, all the more so in the midst of suffering and pain. It is not the fruit of our wishes or of the intense exercise of our thoughts.

This is the horizon that beckons the believer: God's will for humanity is eternal life. And guided by this, we advance. There is no guarantee that the road will be smoothly paved and perfectly straight. It's quite possible we'll take some spills. It's likely that we won't know which fork in the road to take at times. Trials along the way are going to cause us doubts in those moments of fatigue and pain (but always better to have a reasonable doubt than a presumptuous faith). "We know that in everything God works for good with those who love him, who are called according to his purpose" (Romans 8:28).

Thy will be done

This is what the apostle Paul wrote concerning the will of God for you and me: "[God] desires all men to be saved and to come to the knowledge of the truth" (1 Timothy 2:4). The will of God is for our good on this earth and for our eternal salvation. "And the world passes away, and the lust of it; but he who does the will of God abides for ever" (1 John 2:17). The will of God is reflected in the Ten Commandments. Ellen White wrote, "The will of God is expressed in the precepts of His holy law, and the principles of this law are the principles of heaven."[2]

What do we mean by this reference to the Ten Commandments? Can we observe them as we observe traffic laws or any other rules governing the social life? The law of God is profound. The law of God is expressed in the Ten Commandments but is not limited to them. The law of God is the character of God, and the Bible tells us that "God is love" (1 John 4:8). Therefore, the law is love, and it encompasses the entire Word of God—all of His will for man—all that He said in the Old Testament and all that He said in the New Testament. But all of that still does not exhaust the law of God.

The law circulates throughout the Lord's Prayer. This masterful prayer composed by Jesus covers both the vertical relationship between God and man (the first three invocations) as well as the horizontal relationship between man and fellow man (the last four implorations).* This is how Jesus thought of His prayer. The thoughts of Christ were structured on the law. But the law extends before, after, and beyond the Decalogue and the Lord's Prayer. Its principles are eternal. Ellen White expresses it this way: "After the transgression of Adam the principles of the law were . . . definitely arranged and expressed to meet man in his fallen condition."[3]

This means that in the context of universal history, and throughout eternity, the Ten Commandments could be considered as a fairly late development. You don't have to think too hard to reach the conclusion that the law as expressed in the Ten Commandments is an adaptation of the universal principle of God's love manifested toward the human condition. I can't imagine the Lord ever saying to the angels: "You shall not covet your neighbor's wife nor steal their belongings." The same can be deduced about each of the other specific commandments in Exodus 20. This means that the Decalogue cannot and should not be obeyed in the same way we obey traffic laws, employing our own exclusive willpower. It is essential to not confuse the letter of the commandments with the spirit of the law.

The principle of love underlies the Ten Commandments. For that reason, when Jesus was asked by certain learned Jews about the law, He replied, "You shall love the Lord your God with all your heart, and with all your soul, and with all your mind. This is the great and first commandment. And a second is like it, You shall love your neighbor as yourself. On these two commandments depend all the law and the prophets" (Matthew 22:37–40).

But He went on to add: "Woe to you, scribes and Pharisees, hypocrites! For you tithe mint and dill and cummin, and have neglected the weightier matters of the law, justice and mercy and faith; these you ought to have done, without neglecting the others" (Matthew 23:23).

This means that the Ten Commandments are not annulled by love. Love never erases the letter of the law but magnifies it and gives it life. Paul raises a question

---

* See at the end of the chapter, the table that shows the parallel between the Ten Commandments and the Lord's Prayer.

and then immediately answers it: "Do we then overthrow the law by this faith? By no means! On the contrary, we uphold the law" (Romans 3:31). "Love does no wrong to a neighbor; therefore love is the fulfilling of the law" (Romans 13:10).

The law of God is the horizon that guides believers in the way they should go. As the horizon defines physical space, God's law defines spiritual space. We'll never arrive at the horizon; but without it, we are lost. We are perfect before God when we walk looking at that horizon.

> Blessed are those whose way is blameless,
>   who walk in the law of the LORD! (Psalm 119:1).

The law of God is not an instruction manual. The letter does not exhaust its deep spiritual meaning. The more we obey it, the more aware we are of our sinfulness. Similarly, as we advance toward the horizon, the farther away it is.

> Oh, how I love thy law!
>   It is my meditation all the day (verse 97).

In other words, God's will for humanity is that we all might be saved. We can say with the psalmist:

> "I delight to do thy will, O my God;
>   thy law is within my heart" (Psalm 40:8).

For the law of God to be in our hearts, Christ must enter into us. Jesus said, "I am the vine, you are the branches. He who abides in me, and I in him, he it is that bears much fruit, for apart from me you can do nothing" (John 15:5).

On earth as in heaven

The Lord's Prayer reminds us that we are not alone in the universe and that we depend on others and others depend on us. When we pray, "Thy will be done, on earth as it is in heaven," we include the world in this request. It is on the earth where we find our neighbors.

It is the same thing when we ask for our daily bread; we do so not just for ourselves but for others as well. By including others, we pledge to do the will of God in relation to our neighbors.

The closeness of God is never more real than in the face of another human being.

The closeness of God is not expressed in the soul by a feeling of satisfaction. How much hypocrisy is contained in my heart when I feel that God is pleased with me! The closeness of God has nothing to do with human subjectivity, although it is the sounding board of the higher emotions aroused by awareness of the Most High. The closeness of God always, always, always is revealed in the face of the person who needs me. That face never makes me feel satisfied. It disturbs me, it calls to me, it worries me. And this disquieting concern feels only temporary relief when I come to its aid.

Definitively, John says, "He who does not love does not know God; for God is love. . . . Beloved, if God so loved us, we also ought to love one another. No man has ever seen God; if we love one another, God abides in us and his love is perfected in us" (1 John 4:8, 11, 12).

Finally, the believer's hope is that the will of God shall be fulfilled throughout the universe. Ellen White says, "The petition, 'Thy will be done in earth, as it is in heaven,' is a prayer that the reign of evil on this earth may be ended, that sin may be forever destroyed, and the kingdom of righteousness be established. Then in earth as in heaven will be fulfilled 'all the good pleasure of His goodness.' "4

The Lord's Prayer sums up the Law of God

The Lord's Prayer, it can be said, reflects the law of God condensed by the Master for our hearts and prayer guidance. Its seven supplications (seven denotes perfection) recap and abridge the Ten Commandments. The Lord's Prayer presents the Ten Commandments in a positive format compared to the negative wording employed in the Old Testament. The Lord's Prayer aids the Christian believer to focus trust in the Father's love and grace as enshrined in the principles of eternal law.

This prayer demonstrates a harmonic correspondence to the Ten Commandments. Of the seven supplications in the Lord's Prayer, the first three relate to man's relationship to God, just as is the case with the first four commandments. Likewise, the four concluding supplications relate to man's relationships with his fellow man, as well as the final six commandments.

Consider this parallel as clarified in the following table.

LAW OF GOD	THE LORD'S PRAYER
	"Our Father in heaven,"
"Teacher, which is the greatest commandment in the Law?" Jesus replied: " 'Love the Lord your God with all your heart and with all your soul and with all your mind.' This is the first and greatest commandment" (Matthew 22:36–38, NIV).	1. "hallowed be your name," 2. "your kingdom come," 3. "your will be done, on earth as it is in heaven" (Matthew 6:9, 10, NIV).
"And the second is like it: 'Love your neighbor as yourself' " (Matthew 22:39, NIV).	4. "Give us today our daily bread." 5. "Forgive us our debts, as we also have forgiven our debtors." 6. "And lead us not into temptation," 7. "But deliver us from the evil one" (Matthew 6:11–13, NIV).

We can say with Jesus: "On these seven supplications hang all the law and the prophets" (see Mathew 22:40).

Consider the following analytical comparison between the Lord's Prayer and the Ten Commandment Law found in Exodus 20.

THE TEN COMMANDMENTS	THE LORD'S PRAYER
	"Our Father in heaven"
1. "You shall have no other gods before me" (verse 3, NIV).	1. "hallowed be your name,"
2. "You shall not make for yourself an idol in the form of anything in heaven above or on the earth beneath or in the waters below" (verse 4, NIV).	2. "your kingdom come,"
3. "You shall not misuse the name of the LORD your God, for the LORD will not hold anyone guiltless who misuses his name" (verse 7, NIV).	3. "your will be done, on earth as it is in heaven" (Mathew 6:9, 10, NIV).

These three expressions declare the spirit of the first four commandments: God is the Creator, so we sanctify his name, not misusing his name, and observe the Sabbath (see the third and fourth commandments).

Our hope is focused on His kingdom both of grace and of glory; and we do His will (through Christ's merits), as instructed in His law, because there is no other God (first commandment) or anyone else like Him on earth (second commandment).

4. "Remember the Sabbath day by keeping it holy. Six days you shall labor and do all your work, but the seventh day is a Sabbath to the LORD your God" (verses 8–10, NIV).	4. "Give us today our daily bread."
5. "Honor your father and your mother, so that you may live long in the land the LORD your God is giving you" (verse 12, NIV).	5. "Forgive us our debts, as we also have forgiven our debtors."
6. "You shall not murder" (verse 13, NIV).	6. "And lead us not into temptation,"
7. "You shall not commit adultery" (verse 14, NIV).	7. "but deliver us from the evil one" (Matthew 6:11–13, NIV).

The last four supplications of the Lord's Prayer correspond to the fifth commandment in the Decalogue: asking God for "our daily bread" is to cast all our dependence upon Him. This also implies remembering and honoring those who gave us life and sustenance during our childhood—our parents.

The last five commandments correspond to the spirit of forgiveness encapsulated in the fifth supplication of the Lord's Prayer; and the desire to cause no harm, anguish, or loss to our neighbor or fellow man (this is reflected in the sixth and seventh supplications of the Lord's Prayer)—love your neighbor.

8. "You shall not steal" (verse 15, NIV).

9. "You shall not give false testimony against your neighbor" (verse 16, NIV).

10. "You shall not covet your neighbor's house. You shall not covet your neighbor's wife, or his manservant or maidservant, his ox or donkey, or anything that belongs to your neighbor" (verse 17, NIV).

FOR YOUR REFLECTION

1. How can we misinterpret God's will?

2. What does 1 Timothy 2:4 mean to you?

3. Is the will of God expressed in the law?

4. How can we obey the law of God and do His will?

---

1. Dante Alighieri, *Paradise,* canto 1, in *The Divine Comedy.*

2. Ellen G. White, *Thoughts From the Mount of Blessing* (Mountain View, CA: Pacific Press®, 1956), 109.

3. Ellen G. White, *God's Amazing Grace* (Hagerstown, MD: Review and Herald, 2004), 131.

4. White, *Thoughts From the Mount of Blessing,* 110.

Chapter 5

Give Us This Day Our Daily Bread

Bread
While brown bread turns golden
upon the crackling red embers
we raise fervent prayers
to God who lavishes so much good upon us.

While the bread bakes golden filled
with love and heavenly blessings
let's unite hungry hearts
around the divine Nazarene,

pronouncing our psalm of praise
spilling forth eternal gratitude
in that blissful melody,

because he once again nourished trust
and declared divine beatitudes
by giving us our daily bread.

—Alfredo Campechano

My mother used to repeat a saying in Spanish, *"orando y con el mazo dando,"* which translates as "praying and hammering away," which is to say we should not just be begging God for help but also working hard to make ends meet. She would say that most often when things weren't going very well financially. "You're going to have to get your bread out on the street, Ricardito [Ricky]." By that she didn't mean I was going to have to go out and work at the tender age of eight or ten. No, those were the going-to-school years. I remember her saying that she wanted to depart this world leaving her boys educated; and in order to do that she "was working like a mule." It got to be practically a litany with her, to the point that sometimes we thought it would be better that she wouldn't sacrifice so much for us.

I always remember that phrase: "You're going to have to get your bread out on the street," her way of telling us that we could not afford to lie around in bed if we wanted to eat. The apostle Paul was in tune with that idea: "If any one will not work, let him not eat" (2 Thessalonians 3:10). In other words, as Mother insisted, we were going to have to be *buscavidas* (go-getters). As a kid, I loved this phrase.

When I wanted to have some money in my pocket and surprise my mother, I would hit the street to see what business I could find. A newspaper boy named Maurente and I became buddies. He would let me have some of his papers so I could hawk them on the buses. He always gave me a generous commission—he had a good heart. It was fun jumping on and off moving buses selling papers. On weekends I sold ladies garments door to door. People would open their doors and smile graciously—they liked to see a young boy out making the effort to earn a living.

One afternoon, while trying to score some sales, I came upon a big, old-fashioned, Spanish-style house with many rooms leading out to a common enclosed courtyard. To my surprise, out of all those doors came Gypsy women. There were only women and children present, as their men had gone to work. Right away a very large woman—I took her to be the Gypsy mamma—with a threatening look came over and loomed over me. I got the impression that she was going to read my fortune whether I wanted her to or not. Pointing at my two bags of merchandise, she signaled for me to hand them over. Then she and the other Gypsy women hurried off to their rooms. I just gulped and stood there; no need to guess what to expect. I'd just been robbed, it seemed, so this was clearly my bad luck day! Turning around, I was just about to bolt through the front door when out came the female alpha, who said to me: "Here are your bags [they were empty] . . . and here is the money." They had bought it all—every last item! What a wake-up call that was for me! Never judge anyone by their appearance.

Those early experiences of my childhood are what gave me a love for canvassing. Every year during the past quarter century, I have spent my vacation days colporteuring. Every year, without fail, I go to the fruit and vegetable fields of California to take Bibles and literature to the farm workers. I delight in doing this, and it makes me feel alive and free as a kid again. How good it is to get away from the stress and responsibilities of adult life and let that inner kid return. Childhood is a state of consciousness that ends when a puddle of water is no longer seen as something to splash in but as an obstacle to skirt around. To me, getting out in the fields is refreshing, and I come alive.

There, in the midst of the nature that speaks to the glory of God, under the morning sun, or at noon, or in the evening, I open the Bible, read a story, and repeat the Lord's Prayer with those workers. I leave them Bibles without any up-front payment, and the farm managers take charge of the billing. Nobody has ever skipped out on paying. Those who work with their hands in the soil are honorable people.

They have another attribute, those farm workers who come from the other side of the border, that dividing line that too often produces dreams on one side and nightmares on the other. These farmhands who work the soil are noble. They will never leave a stranger without food; Pablo Neruda rightly said that there are no people in the world with the depth of a Mexican soul.[1] On every single occasion, without exception, when I have arrived during their mealtimes, they have offered me something first before eating their food. They might talk with their mouths full, but that is not bad; what is bad is to talk with your heart empty.

Bread

This is perhaps the most human of the seven petitions found in the Lord's Prayer, because at a glance we see that it has to do with man's most basic need: food. We live on bread.

Interestingly, the same Lord who urged us not to be overly concerned about having food to eat (see Matthew 6:25) is also the One who inspires in the believer's heart this request: give us our daily bread. He instructs us to ask God to supply this need.

Bread is a very rich symbol in the teachings of Jesus. It is present in the story of Christ when He referred to the manna that fed the people of Israel in the desert, in the miracle of the Sermon on the Mount, and in the Passover. The symbol of bread runs throughout the life story of Christ, the Bread of Life.

We live on bread. Bread is the fruit of the land and the work of man's hand. But the land would not otherwise give its fruit if it did not receive from above sunshine and rain. Bread is the result of a partnership between man and nature, and both depend on God. Work is blessed by health; and health by life, which comes from the Creator. This association of our hands with nature's providence is an antidote to our natural pride, which tries to deceive us with the notion that we can sustain ourselves on this planet by our own means.

We live in an era that turns people proud and self-sufficient. We glorify scientific knowledge, and we admire the technology that bestows on us a comfortable lifestyle, but we forget something basic: it is the earth that gives us what we eat. For this reason, we should take good care of it.

That is why, saying "give us this day our daily bread" is the beginning of humility. In effect, we are saying, "Lord, we cannot do it on our own." To ask for bread is an expression of humility and trust in God: if earthly parents give good gifts, how much more will the Lord do for us (see Luke 11:9–13)! This prayer request expresses our dependence on forces superior to those of nature, which are controlled by the Creator.

Our bread

The possessive pronoun *our* has deep significance, and it is only used once after the invocation of the Lord's Prayer. While all humanity stands as one in need upon the earth, so there is One in heaven who provides for our needs: the Father.

When we ask for our bread, we are also asking for bread for others. "None of us lives to himself, and none of us dies to himself" (Romans 14:7). We are not alone in the universe. Our bread is also the bread of the world. When we ask for our bread, the Lord also says to us: give them to eat. "Then Jesus called his disciples to him and said, 'I have compassion on the crowd, because they have been with me now three days, and have nothing to eat; and I am unwilling to send them away hungry, lest they faint on the way.' . . . He took the seven loaves and the fish, and having given thanks he broke them and gave them to the disciples, and the disciples gave them to the crowds" (Matthew 15:32, 36).

To share bread is God's reply to our request of bread from Him. The apostle James wrote, "If a brother or sister is ill-clad, and in lack of daily food, and one of you says to them, 'Go in peace, be warmed and filled,' without giving them the things needed for the body, what does it profit?" (James 2:15, 16).

We humans are accustomed to separating the different areas of life into airtight compartments: one for work, one for activities with friends, one for household chores, one for sports and recreation; but what about religion? At first glance, it seems to be just another compartment, separated from the others. Isn't it true that we keep it slightly distanced from the different range of relationships with other human beings? So, when it comes to practicing a pure religion, we strive to block out the other areas that might get in between God and our souls. This separation appears to be natural and self-evident.

However, in relation to this matter, we find in the epistle of James a truly unique and amazing verse that just might open our eyes and allow us to rectify our thinking: "Religion that is pure and undefiled before God and the Father is this: to visit orphans and widows in their affliction, and to keep oneself unstained from the world" (James 1:27).

If we think that in order to remain pure and uncontaminated by the world we must separate ourselves from other people, we are quite mistaken. This text says just the opposite. And it is in harmony with the fourth petition in the Lord's Prayer: "Give us this day our daily bread." Ellen White says in regard to this: "When we pray, 'Give us this day our daily bread,' we ask for others as well as ourselves. And we acknowledge that what God gives us is not for ourselves alone. God give to us in trust, that we may feed the hungry. Of His goodness He has prepared for the poor."[2] Attending to the needs of others is not an add-on to religion; to the contrary, it is the essence of pure religion.

We must not look at things with cross-eyed vision—with one eye trying to focus on God and the other on our neighbor. Of course, they are not one and the same, but separating and isolating one from the other is a thing of the past, for Jesus overcame our separation from God by His redemptive death on the cross. What was far off has drawn near, and Jesus has opened the way for us to the Father. Because of His love for Jesus, the Father has touched our hearts, which were once far away from Him, and has transformed them, drawing us towards Him, endowing us with grace and with His Holy Spirit. Through the Holy Spirit, God wants to live in our hearts. He doesn't want to merely live "up there," far above us; because of His love for Jesus, He wants to live in and among us, not just in our churches, but in the living grace that moves in our everyday, secular lives. God inspires in us those desires to be good and to care for our neighbors. God is in those impulses in favor of lives of service that we feel even before we realize where they are coming from (Romans 5:5).

Therefore, when we lend our energies to this calling; when we take care of orphans, widows, and the oppressed; when we share our bread with the poor instead of leaving them without, God is present. And we honor Him, even without His name.

Our daily bread

To ask God for our sustenance is not only necessary but noble.

> I have not seen the righteous forsaken
> or his children begging bread (Psalm 37:25).

This is not just a conviction held by David, it is a divine promise. God moves in the world, lavishing it with blessings. God's desire is for our spiritual well-being as well as our material well-being. It is worth noting that this petition for our daily bread comes after hallowing God's name. The believer who sanctifies His name can expect to receive the daily bread, but he doesn't live by or for that bread alone:

> "Man shall not live by bread alone,

but by every word that proceeds from the mouth of God" (Matthew 4:4).

We may really need some bread, or perhaps we hope for greater prosperity in our lives, but unless we first sanctify God's name, we will live out our lives in this world simply seeking to satisfy our basic needs—a very elementary standard by which to live. Even prosperity is not necessarily a sign of divine blessing. Often, wealth and prosperity are signs of moral decay. The very phrase "Give us this day our daily bread" tells us in effect, "Let the day's own trouble be sufficient for the day" (Matthew 6:34, RSV). Each day signifies what is sufficient for today.

A short story by the Russian writer Varlam Tikhonovich Shalamov (1907–1982) comes to mind. He spent much of his life in a concentration camp under the communist regime, where he wrote the *Kolyma Tales.*

In one of his stories, he writes the following:

> That piece of bread belonged to another, it was my partner's piece of bread. He trusted only me with it. They sent him off to work the day shift and the piece of bread was left in my care. I kept it for him in a little wooden Russian box. There it was that ration of bread in the box. If you shake the box you can hear it sliding around inside. I kept it underneath my head at night but I could not sleep. A hungry man sleeps badly. But I didn't sleep for thinking of that piece of bread; it was not mine, it was my partner's.
>
> I sat on the bunk . . . I counted up to a thousand and rose again. I opened the little box and lifted the piece of bread out. It was a ration of hard tack three hundred grams in weight, as cold as a chunk of wood. Secretly, I brought it up to my nose; there was just a faint smell of bread. I turned the little box over and dumped a few crumbs from it into the palm of my hand. I licked my hand with my tongue. My mouth filled with saliva in an instant. The crumbs melted and dissolved. I ceased hesitating, pinched three croutons off that piece of bread, small as a fingernail, put the rest of the bread in the little wooden box, and lay down again on my bunk. Slowly I sucked on those bread crumbs. I fell asleep, proud of myself for not stealing my partner's bread.[3]

Man does not live by bread alone.

The Bread of Life

In the words *daily bread* there is a hint of the future. The petition concerning "daily bread" brings to mind the forty years of Israel's wandering in the desert when God gave them manna day after day without fail. His promise was sure from the first day and onward all those years.

Then, many centuries later, the desert manna symbolically came to fulfillment in the Last Supper when Jesus broke the bread in representation of His body soon to be broken for our salvation. In Christ, the biblical figure of the bread reaches its essential meaning. Jesus is our Bread. With Him culminates the physical and spiritual interchange between heaven and earth. He is the Bread of Life; it was He who fed His people in the past, and He will feed His people for all eternity.

Jesus said, "I am the living bread which came down from heaven; if anyone eats of this bread, he will live for ever; and the bread which I shall give for the life of the world is my flesh" (John 6:51).

> The prayer for daily bread includes not only food to sustain the body, but that spiritual bread which will nourish the soul unto life everlasting. . . . Our Saviour is the bread of life, and it is by beholding His love, by receiving it into the soul, that we feed upon the bread which came down from heaven. . . .
>
> In teaching us to ask every day for what we need—both temporal and spiritual blessings—God has a purpose to accomplish for our good. . . . He is seeking to draw us into communion with Himself. In this communion with Christ, through prayer and the study of the great and precious truths of His word, we shall as hungry souls be fed.[4]

FOR YOUR REFLECTION

1. What does the expression "our daily bread" mean?

2. What does the expression "daily" mean?

3. What significance do the words of John 6:51 have for you?

4. How can Christ be our Bread of Life?

1. Pablo Neruda, *Confieso que he vivido.*
2. White, *Thoughts From the Mount of Blessing,* 111, 112.
3. Varlam Tikhonovich Shalamov, *Relatos de Kolimá,* 461, 462.
4. White, *Thoughts From the Mount of Blessing,* 112, 113.

Chapter 6

Forgive Us Our Debts, as We Also Have Forgiven Our Debtors

I Do Not Blame or Forgive You
You anticipated your destiny
You fulfilled your prophecy
Your own story
That is to say the same

You could not with the old
With what was
With what has been
And as in a litany
The instant future always
the same

And the monotone convinced you of the
Absence of your parent
And you were left without hope
Without strategy
With only enchantment
Without breaking the spell

So I do not blame or forgive you
You did what you could
I never asked you for anything
Not for a bit of fruit
Nor a piece of bread

And you bequeathed me your absence
That you thought was unimportant

But it was definitive

And today brought abandonment
As always
Like a sign
With little peace
And with much luck

But in the dead of night
When time doesn't
Take responsibility for anything
It makes no sense

I am summoned by the Word
By him who wrote out of nothing
That is to say ex nihilo
And it was in its beginning
The first verb
New Man

And for an instant
I was clothed in hope
I leap from myself
To where you are
Where I am
Looking for a shelter
Looking for a coat

And the absence becomes
Less definitive
The depths greet one another
Fellow companions
What is lacking is understanding
A shared emotion

And for a moment
Almost forever
I thank you
Because I become a father
Lord of myself.

—Ricardo Bentancur

The history of every man is defined by the way in which he resolves his relationship with his father. This was certainly true in my case.

My father left home when I was just five years old. The verses that precede this chapter were written when I was an adult but before my father died. They reflect the mental quest that marked my childhood and adolescence; the poetic progression testifies to a reconciliation within as I entered my mature years. They were composed, I can almost say, with the speed of a sneeze, but the underlying virus did its harm during the decades. These verses served as an act of liberation, a catharsis. This was my way of swearing before the world that the story of my progenitor would not repeat itself in me. I was absolutely determined to break this curse; no reoccurring cycle of trauma such as I experienced would be allowed in the succeeding generation if I could possibly help it. This was the issue: to change history; and faith was the catalyst for success.

Faith was the greatest gift from God in those years of my childhood. It came from the hand of a Seventh-day Adventist nurse who helped my mother give birth to me in the old apartment where she lived, because there was no time to get to the hospital. That midwife who assisted at the birth of hundreds of children shared her faith with my mother, and years later, when my father left us, was like a lifeguard who rescued her from turbulent waters.

I once read that women are the only beings capable of thinking with the heart, acting from their emotions, and overcoming by love. To think with the heart, yes, convincingly, that is the power of a woman. Blaise Pascal, the French philosopher, said it well: "The heart has its reasons, which reason does not know."[1] I have never seen anyone in the world who has enjoyed even the smallest flicker of happiness without having lived a passion produced in the heart. Reason preserves us from the evils of this existence, but passion ignites the sacred flame of life, which is love. I once read that life is not measured by how many times we breathe, but by those moments that take our breath away. Reason can count the number of times we inhale and exhale, but passion leaves us breathless.

There are all kinds of passions: those that destroy, and those that rescue the soul from its pit of sorrows. Since my mother accepted the faith that came by the testimony of that midwife, her passion for Jesus Christ rescued her from death. And with that passion for life given to her, faith took charge of everything: in our poverty, we never lacked food, books, or an example of incorruptible character. Mother never gave up. She always worked hard; she never abandoned my brother and me.

My old resentment

According to the dictionary, *resentment* means "a feeling of anger or displeasure about someone or something unfair." Resentment is a bitter and deeply rooted memory of a particular injury, for which one wishes to extract satisfaction. In other words, resentment is a festering toxic memory.

According to psychologist Dr. Luis Kancyper, the term *resentment* comes from the Latin *rancor*, meaning complaint, quarrel, demand, and is derived from the Latin root *rancidus*. The Spanish term *rencoroso* comes from the same root and is related to two other very significant words in Spanish: *rancio* (rancid) and *rengo* (cripple; lame). This etymology describes two hallmarks of resentment: the condition of something old and spoiled, which is to say stale; and the other means being stuck, immobile, not able to get around because of the pain it causes.[2]

Julio Sosa, a famous singer of Uruguayan tangos from the mid-twentieth century, sings with remarkable expressiveness a song about a person who holds an old grudge. His lyrics are wrenching:

> This cursed hate that I carry in my veins embitters my life like a sentence of
>   condemnation;
> the wrong done to me is an open wound,
> which fills my heart with rage and gall.
> My eyes hate her because they have seen her;
> my lips hate her because they have kissed her.
> I hate her with all the strength of my soul,
> and my hate is as great as my love once was.

At times, his hatred intensifies and becomes a passion for revenge:

> I hope to God one day to find her still alive,
> crying and overcome by her wretched past,
> so I can dump on her all this contempt,
> that has fouled my heart with bitter resentment.

But the protagonist suffers "a doubt that burns in his breast," and with an outburst of sincerity, admits:

> Never repeat what I tell you.
> Resentment, I fear that you might be love.

Then we realize that the great inner conflict of this resentment is a struggle between love and hate, the hate one feels so intensely due to frustrated love.

After reading the lyrics of this tango, non-Hispanic readers might begin to grasp an underlying quirk in the Hispanic psyche. (Or in the psyche of all humankind?)

Sometimes resentment emerges from disappointed or betrayed love. Other times it is stirred up by envy, cowardice, feelings of humiliation, or of nonconformity with oneself, among other things. The fact is that when we are thus ensnared, we feel terribly irritated, we practically taste its bitterness in our mouths, and time and again we mull over the searing memory of the offense.

We teeter between doing violence and keeping the lid on our torn and conflicted egos. Around and around it goes, the mind morbidly regurgitating the same old hateful disgusts in order to keep the grudge from dying. Resentment is a trap devised by disgrace. It is that place where the will falters and calm thinking is tossed to the wind. It is the shadowy place of the mind where wretchedness, contempt, and haplessness try their hardest to destroy the soul.

Resentment and society

Resentments lie at the heart of many wars. The ongoing conflicts between Jews and Arabs arise from deep resentments since ancient times. My Hispanic ethnicity bears witness to deep cultural roots in resentments. If that is not so, then why do we put each other down so disgracefully?

"Numskull, donkey, dunderhead" were some of the first adjectives I learned in my early childhood. I heard those harsh insults from my older brother's fifth-grade teacher. I guess she thought our vocabulary needed "enrichment." When my brother came home from school, he would ask Mother what that day's new words meant.

"What does *numskull* mean, Mamma? What does *dunderhead* mean?"

"Where did you hear that?"

"From my teacher; she said I was a numskull and a dunderhead because I didn't know the lesson."

Mother burned with anger.

Those were simply a few of many such insulting expressions typical to our Hispanic culture. We feed on such sayings as *"la letra con sangre entra"* (learning enters with blood). There is this notion that we have to suffer in order to learn. We fail to heed Solomon's wise warning: "When words are many, transgression is not lacking" (Proverbs 10:19). Even at home we throw around cutting expressions like knives to defend ourselves. Nicknames such as traitor, lame, one-eyed, and one-armed are used to refer even to our friends. It seems we take glee in accentuating physical defects or weaknesses in others. There is a made-up Spanish term for this kind of behavior: *ninguneamos,* which means we make others as nothing. We test the patience of our closest peers by flinging at them these hurtful ironies.

We laugh at others' pain. Fear is the weapon of choice for teachers, politicians, and particularly, religious leaders.

Just as the teacher insults the students, so a father his son, a husband his wife, and a politician the people; nobody is innocent. How many times have I hurt my daughters with my ironies! Not long ago, my oldest daughter, tired of my Hispanic ironies, spoke back: "Dad, enough already! No one has hurt my feelings in life as much as you."

I was taken aback like never before. This Bible text took on new meaning for me:

You are snared by the words of your mouth;
You are taken by the words of your mouth (Proverbs 6:2, NKJV).

The sanctuary: The place of forgiveness

How can we ever rightly esteem others if we do not first respect ourselves? How can we forgive if we are not forgiven? My people, the Hispanic, are children of sorrow; we are a mass of muscle, blood, and dust. The vast majority of us come from poor societies, broken homes, and close-up acquaintance with violence and pain for several generations.

The most important questions to ask are, How can we escape the snare of resentment where so many are entrapped? How do we overcome bitterness and the desire for revenge? An antidote is needed for this powerful soul poison. The answer is found in the antonym for *spite,* and that is *forgiveness.* Jorge Luis Borges said that forgiveness ennobles the victim, but it can leave the pardoned one unchanged. This is so because forgiveness frees us within from the torture of self-accusation, from its accompanying reproach, and from desires for revenge. It quenches the thirst for retaliation. Forgiveness reduces words to silence; it illuminates the dark side of the heart; and it frees us from the painful bonds of the past. Forgiveness can lead to reconciliation with others, but more importantly, it leads to reconciliation within oneself.

Our emotions are not changed by decree. Scars remain. But wounds cease bleeding and begin to heal with forgiveness. Forgiveness is primarily an act of the will; but the will must be illuminated and fortified.

Where do we go to find the strength to forgive? Believers are convinced that God's help is needed to produce the miracle of softened hearts once these are hardened by resentment. That miracle will produce a blissful feeling of release. When we receive God's forgiveness for our contemptibility, it then becomes easier for us to forgive others. "And be kind to one another, tenderhearted, forgiving one another, as God in Christ forgave you" (Ephesians 4:32).

God is love. His forgiveness is available to us every day of our lives. The experience of receiving forgiveness is what enables us to grant it. This amplifies the words of the Lord's Prayer: Father, "forgive us . . . , as we also have forgiven our debtors" (Matthew 6:12).

The best representation of forgiveness is the earthly sanctuary and the heavenly sanctuary. The day Jesus died, the priest who officiated in the temple courts at Jerusalem was just at the point of offering a sacrificial lamb. When the priest raised the knife to kill the victim, the earth shook violently. Terrified, the priest dropped the knife, and the lamb escaped.[3] The inner veil was torn at that same moment (Matthew 27:51). Across the city, on Golgotha, black clouds shrouded the cross of Christ. Jesus, the true Passover Lamb, then exclaimed, "It is finished" (Luke 19:30). He died for the sins of the world. The very event long pointed to in the earthly sanctuary services had at last taken place. The Savior had completed His atoning sacrifice; thus, ritual symbolism was overtaken in real time by Messianic fulfillment. In that precise moment, the shadowy figures of the past ended. That is why the veil was torn asunder and the lamb escaped. Humankind's separation from God ended.

However, the history of salvation reaches beyond the cross. The resurrection and ascension of Jesus direct our attention to the heavenly sanctuary, where Christ, the eternal Lamb of God, conducts His high priestly role. "So Christ was offered once to bear the sins of many" (Hebrews 9:28, NKJV). He now offers the benefits of this atoning sacrifice, making it available to all. This is divine justice satisfied by His sacrifice. Divine forgiveness is thus guaranteed to humanity. Christ's sacrifice is the price paid for forgiveness.

The New Testament reveals that Jesus now serves as High Priest "at the right hand of the throne of the Majesty" in the heavenly sanctuary. The sanctuary is the "true tabernacle, which the Lord pitched, and not man" (Hebrews 8:1, 2, KJV). The heavenly sanctuary is not a metaphor; it is real. It is the primary abode of God. Three phases of Christ's ministry are carried forward in that sanctuary: (1) the benefits of His substitutionary sacrifice are applied, (2) priestly mediation is offered, and (3) the final judgment is conducted. It is the great work of divine justice to ensure God's forgiveness to humanity. This eternal truth is given so that we might know that we are forgiven and that it is now our turn to forgive those who have offended us.

The resolution of a life

When you are a child, standing barely three or four feet tall, it is no fun having your world crash down around you. A child should not have to bear the hatred unleashed when parents divorce—that little one is faultless and owes them no "pound of flesh." When he becomes an adult, that will be his time to bear account for the impact his actions have on the next generation. There is no "right" by which a child's innocence is taken away. That is the rising sap that allows the little one to grow with some degree of confidence in himself and in others. But such is life, and when two adults cannot agree to protect their children, the damage they inflict can be irreparable.

Those childhood years my brother and I experienced left us with insecurities. My transgressions, low self-esteem, and feelings of guilt were sometimes excruciating, no matter how unfounded they might have been. I sought to please others to the point that it overly prejudiced my own well-being. And, like millions and millions who inhabit this planet, I tried to find in those early years of confusion some answer from my father. I just wanted to understand why I received such indifference from him. I had never had a deep emotional encounter with him. I sought that, but it never happened. It wasn't that he didn't want the same; it's most likely that he just wasn't able to offer it. His life was also marked by the abandonment of his father, my grandfather.

With that burden weighing on my heart, at eighteen, at an age when little makes sense, I cried out in the darkness of my night, "God, if You exist, make Yourself known in my soul." And He who made everything from nothing put in my heart these words that I carry with me ever since: "I will take you in My arms, and I will teach you to walk" (see Hosea 11:3).

Years passed; I traveled to the city where my father lived with his new wife and son to say Goodbye to him; I was getting ready to travel with my family to the United States. Standing there in front of his house, something stopped me. "Aren't you going to go in?" my eldest daughter asked. "No, let's come back a few days before we leave." Two weeks later, I received a phone call at our home; my half brother broke the news: "Dad is dead." His end came not long after I had gone to see him but couldn't bring myself to knock on his door. He was cremated; his absence was final, but my love for him has not faltered.

Dear reader, if you are struggling under a heavy burden, perhaps a grudge that embitters your life, if you feel you can no longer bear this life, pray to God:

"Forgive us our debts,
    As we also have forgiven our debtors" (Matthew 6:12).

Release your past with all its suffering into His arms. Your resentment will turn to understanding and hope.

FOR YOUR REFLECTION

1. What is the definition of *resentment*?

2. What do Proverbs 6:2 and 10:19 mean to you?

3. According to the sanctuary doctrine, what relation is there between divine and human forgiveness? Read Matthew 6:15.

4. What does "forgive us our debts" in Matthew 6:12 mean?

------

1. Blaise Pascal, *Pensées,* note 277.

2. Luis Kancyper, *Resentimiento y Remordimiento,* 17.

3. Ellen G. White, *The Desire of Ages,* (Mountain View, CA: Pacific Press®, 1940), 756, 757.

Chapter 7

Lead Us Not Into Temptation

Temptation
The temptation, a bother of Odysseus,
Armed with delicious complacency
Of ardor and superficiality in appearance
Also followed the footsteps of the Hebrew.

Lit with the fire of desire
The temptation dressed licentiously
Vestal of seductive of incontinence
Blinded Samson, used him as a trophy.

Therefore we pray to you, Nazarene,
Protect us from the fire of the hour
Of sweet temptation and its evil

From its power and its gall and venom
Help us by your beneficent hand
By the everlasting love of our Father.

—Alfredo Campechano

I do not like to talk about temptation, not because it is a sin, but because somehow it reveals my inner weaknesses, my personal areas of conflict and struggle. I do not want anyone to see my shortcomings, let alone my vileness; I do not want to be exposed. Failure produces a revulsion that drives away even those nearest to us. Each one of us is set on success; nobody deliberately aims for defeat. We skirt around the fallen in silence, discreetly and modestly to be sure, but keeping as far away as possible.

It is difficult for believers to admit that we are weak. Moreover, we like to think that our leaders are perfect, or ought to be. We feel let down when they fall. These past days my heart, as a pastor, suffered a terrible blow when a colleague committed suicide. How is it possible that a religious leader would yield to the temptation of death? Should suicide be seen as a temptation in the life of a man, or is it more like a last cry of desperation?

What became of his faith? The pain seemed more poignant because of the silence of almost all of his fellow pastors at the Web site where the news first aired. Only one or two wrote a message of condolence to the family. And there was one who tried to justify the silence: better to keep silent so as to not cause additional "shame to the deceased pastor's loved ones." Then arose the voice of an older, more experienced pastor of souls, who wrote, "Yes, of course it is edifying to speak clearly and with dignity about what has happened. We are masters of concealment and make-believe, and in part that is why things like this happen. I do not personally know the deceased, nor do I have any additional information to add, but how does a pastor go about telling others he is depressed and is experiencing suicidal thoughts? With whom would he dare to speak of such things? Are you ashamed? Just imagine how it was for him! Let the truth be clear but dignified, that way we can recognize that we are merely humans and not supermen. We must pray for our pastors, they are the most solitary people on earth."

"No man is matriculated to the art of life till he has been well tempted," wisely pondered the English writer George Eliot.[1]

I know about this matter of falling into temptation. And the apostle Paul also knew about it. He opened up his heart and let it all pour forth: "For I know that nothing good dwells within me, that is, in my flesh. I can will what is right, but I cannot do it. For I do not do the good I want, but the evil I do not want is what I do. Now if I do what I do not want, it is no longer I that do it, but sin which dwells within me" (Romans 7:18–20).

Subject to the power of temptation, one might conclude that the only way to overcome its attraction is by giving in to it. Oscar Wilde said, with a degree of irony, that effectively this was the best way to deal with it. But that is wrong; in fact, it is quite to the contrary. Its destructive power is limitless. To slip into temptation leaves us far from the path of righteousness. It becomes very difficult then to pick up and get back on track. Only with sacrifice and much suffering is it possible to get back on the right path. Even so, it is the only healthy and mature thing to do. Still, it is a comfort to remember that He who loves the most is the most willing to forgive. Every fall into sin leaves a scar; but aren't these scars the marks that give stature and dignity to a warrior?

After his double sin of adultery and murder, the poet and king David declared:

Have mercy on me, O God, according to thy steadfast love;
    according to thy abundant mercy blot out my transgressions.
Wash me thoroughly from my iniquity,
    and cleanse me from my sin!

For I know my transgressions,
    and my sin is ever before me. . . .
Behold, I was brought forth in iniquity,
    and in sin did my mother conceive me (Psalm 51:1–3, 5).

And then upon receiving the forgiveness of his heavenly Father, he offered this praise:

O my Strength, I will sing praises to thee,
    for thou, O God, art my fortress,
    the God who shows me steadfast love (Psalm 59:17).

For thy steadfast love is great to the heavens (Psalm 57:10).

The unknown God

Temptation is like bait that is so transparent the hook can clearly be seen; nevertheless, we approach it eagerly and take the bait. It is truly amazing how we give ourselves to self-destruction.

I don't think there's a single person in this world who doesn't have to endure temptation, and that includes atheists. While we may deny the existence of God, sin, and judgment, we cannot deny our human frailty and weakness. Everyone has a moral conscience that whispers good and bad things. Temptation is universal; it draws people like moths to a glowing flame. The fire of evildoing will burn all who venture too close. Its effects can also singe innocent bystanders. All human beings are exposed to wickedness. We are born with this tendency toward evil, which nourishes temptation (Psalm 51:5).

Just as every human being has a unique fingerprint, each one also has personally tailored temptations. Mine was to follow in the path of my father and grandfather, repeating the misfortunes of their lives. This would have left me more or less an isolated recluse. It seemed as if they had marked out a path and a destiny that all their succeeding generations must follow, leading to a solitary existence and demise.

To break the mandate of that old story and to write my own new one was something that could be achieved only with the help of God.

By saying I could do that *only* "with the help of God" might sound a little conceited on my part. It's as if my self-interest prompts me to tie up God's attention so completely that everybody else gets put on hold with their own urgent situations and pleas unattended. It sounds a bit arrogant of me, but it really isn't. I will explain.

I have personally known people who went through terrible experiences or, like me, received tragic or nonexistent role-modeling from their ancestors. These affected ones never turned to God for help because they were atheists. As I said above, writing a new life story is possible only with the help of God, and by this I mean that it is God who gives us the strength to change the outcome even when we do not recognize the source of empowerment or believe in Him, for that matter. For it is written, "Every good endowment and every perfect gift is from above, coming down from the Father of lights with whom there is no variation or shadow due to change" (James 1:17). If you receive a gift from God, it is not because you're so wonderful and special, better than anyone else. Leave the evaluations and the distribution of gifts to Him. If you receive something good from God, it is because He loves you despite yourself. You don't have to deserve anything; that's the way it works with His love. There are times when you won't know where the strength and drive are coming from.

I was about twelve years old when I first read Plato's *Apology* of Socrates. I was by no means a child prodigy. It is a book that any boy of eleven or twelve can read. It's a simple, beautiful, moving work and yet profound. I carried that book with me the day my mother took me to the Rosenblat home. They were a Jewish family who had emigrated from postwar Germany. In Mother's eyes, the Rosenblats were a very rich family. They lived in a posh residential section of Montevideo. My mother spent hours there each week cleaning their house, which overlooked the estuary of the River Plate, called a sea by my countrymen. Before heading to the Rosenblat home, my mother clued me in on how to behave: "Do not talk, sit upright in the chair, and respond only when they ask you something." It almost seemed as if Mrs. Rosenblat was as important as the queen of England. But no, she was a sweet old lady who welcomed me graciously into their home and offered me tea and a book so that I would not be bored while my mother worked. When she saw that I had a book in my hands, she showed interest in it. Next she engaged me in conversation about philosophy. I still remember her aristocratic manners, which reminded me of fine china and gave an elegant touch to her conversation. It was a delight; she didn't speak down to me because I was a child. She answered all my questions (although my mother had warned me not to ask anything). Mrs. Rosenblat was a survivor of a Nazi concentration camp. I could not help but ask her about that. She related that story to me, and at its conclusion, I asked her whether she thanked God for having spared her life during the war. She looked out the window toward the sea and then she spoke in a sweet voice: "It was luck, Ricardo."

"Why?"

My question came from a background of comments I had heard in my neighborhood: the Catholics said that the Jews were atheists. So I posed her another question: "Don't you believe in God?"

Her answer was as laconic and to the point. It took me years to digest it.

"Why should I believe in a God who saves some and forgets others?"

It was too much for my preteen ears that a Jewish person could tell me that she didn't feel privileged. After all, hadn't it been the Jews who invented the idea of a chosen people?

There is in a human being a tremendous capacity to survive in extreme situations. There are atheists with remarkable inner strength, superior even to some believers. Atheism is an option in the heart of man, because God gave everyone the freedom to believe or not to believe. The point is that all the good that comes to us comes from the Father of lights. Everyone should give Him thanks. Some do, and others do not. Some are even convinced that they have good reasons not to believe. But God made the sun to shine upon everyone, for those who believe and also for those who do not (see Matthew 5:45).

In the concentration camps, the atheistic existentialism of Sartre was born. But there also germinated the thoughts of two great believers: the philosopher Emmanuel Levinas and the psychiatrist Viktor Frankl. Their thoughts left a profound mark on philosophy and Christian theology in the second half of the twentieth century. How true is the saying that "the same heat that softens wax, hardens clay"![2] (This discussion raises the question of the origin of evil and God's responding action, which we will discuss in chapter 8.)

The apostle Paul, in the Acts of the Apostles, speaks about the God of lights that man does not know or recognize. On one of his missionary journeys, Paul visited Athens. While walking through the center of the city, his "spirit was provoked within him as he saw that the city was full of idols" (Acts 17:16). For that reason, "he argued in the synagogue with the Jews and devout persons, and in the market place every day with those who chanced to be there" (verse 17). Some philosophers who heard him speak invited him to meet with them up on the Areopagus, a hilltop location where the Athenians gathered to discuss philosophy and politics (verses 18, 19). It is interesting to consider why the philosophers invited Paul to explain his doctrine:

"May we know what this new teaching is which you present? For you bring some strange things to our ears; we wish to know therefore what these things mean." Now all the Athenians and the foreigners who lived there spent their time in nothing except telling or hearing something new.

So Paul, standing in the middle of the Areopagus, said: "Men of Athens, I perceive that in every way you are very religious. For as I passed along, and observed the objects of your worship, I found also an altar with this inscription, 'To an unknown god.' What therefore you worship as unknown, this I proclaim to you" (verses 19–23).

The unknown God embraces and blesses all humankind. Because of His love, He acts in the lives of people without their even knowing it.

Navigation

Going back to my time of torment, in those difficult days I wrote my first book, *Contra viento y marea* (Against wind and sea), in which I referred to storms and torments—two words with only one letter difference in Spanish (*tormentas* and *tormentos*), but with vastly different meanings. A person can be in the midst of the severest trials of life, but if he or she is standing on Christ the Rock, those raging winds will not prevail. But if a person is tormented, destroyed within, it won't take much of a breeze at all to bring him or her crashing down. Some live in the midst of torments without ever having gone through a storm. If your personal storm is one of internal torments, Jesus invites you: "Come unto me, all ye that labor and are heavy laden, and I will give you rest" (Matthew 11:28, KJV).

At that time in my own tormented life, I wrote these verses, which I titled "Navigation":

> Sometimes the ship sails
> Weathering the tempest
> And it sets leeward
> Wise and stripped of sails
> Drenched in courage
> It ponders how to handle
> The wind
> It knows what to do with
> The ship
> One should snatch its
> Secret
>
> Sometimes the ship sails

Battered
It sails are slack
Draining on the starboard
A certain liquid
Its very own life
But it still leaves a wake
And perhaps that is why
It causes us little worry

Sometimes the ship sails
In an agitated state
And Eros is tormented
And the moral order is confused
With the natural order
And one needs to be tied to the main mast
Like Ulysses
Or cover the eyes
And the ears
Like the sailors

Sometimes the ship sails
Under double sails
Majestic
And the ship
Sails forth joyfully
And with
Skyriver riversky
Finally
It reconciles
And the ship sails on.

Life is a rough sea with turbulent waters. Amid the trials, confusion, and temptation, God gives us wisdom to convert those winds into the driving force of our ship. He makes known to us that our suffering is not in vain. He strengthens us against temptation, and He fortifies our hope with the assurance that a better day is coming.

There is nothing more rewarding than to write one's own story. Nothing is more satisfying than to change the story others thought to impose on us. We are not mindless actors simply performing according to a script written for us by an unknown author. Instead, we are participants in a story God is writing with and for us. No conquest is greater than the overcoming of our own frailties. God was my Refuge and my life Companion who never let go of my hand. That is why I can now write these lines.

It was a Friday late in the afternoon; I remember it as if it yesterday, although in reality a number of years have passed. Florencia, my wife, said she wanted to talk to me. At the time I was in my midlife crisis, to give you a hint as to what was unfolding. The tone of her voice alerted me that it was something serious. Those had been difficult days, although for Florencia her gauges read them as difficult years. I think she had a better grip on the reality of time. So, we sat down together in the kitchen to talk. She looked me straight in the eye and spoke her mind: "If you do not change, we cannot continue to live together." The calmness with which she articulated those words made me shift position in my chair several times. She spoke calmly, without any anger. A word to the wise: pay close attention when somebody speaks to you seriously without anger.

Florencia was tired of my crises; she couldn't deal with both hers and mine much longer. We humans live through crises throughout our years. Psychologists are good at classifying them, as if by this they can exorcise them: the weaning crisis, adolescent crisis, middle-age crisis, old-age crisis—we live in crisis. Many of these are natural consequences of the growing-up process.

When Florencia didn't express what she felt but what she thought, I felt the earth move under my feet. It wasn't "mom Florencia" speaking but rather, my wife. (All men look for mothers in their wives, and that is why men can get so abusive towards them.) I knew, as the French say, when a man takes a radical stand with regard to his wife, a problem begins; but when a woman does the same to her husband, the problem is about to be solved. Florencia is a woman of few words and far from what Schopenhauer thought about females—that they have long hair and short ideas. My wife has very long ideas, and lately, short hair. Here, as in good poetry, the silent spaces can often say more than the words. Florencia is like that, a woman of silence (at least when not overly perturbed).

When she finished speaking her mind, she asked me to go to the store across the street and buy two pounds of tomatoes. I never obeyed more quickly. I was confused. I crossed San Martin Avenue in Buenos Aires, which was a very busy two-way street, without seeing the cars and buses speeding by. I don't even know how I got across in my daze. I bought two pounds of potatoes and returned home. When I set down my purchase, Florencia reacted immediately: "Look what you brought me! Didn't I tell you that you never pay attention to me?" I guess that for too many years I had not paid enough attention. And besides that, I had burdened her with all my crises.

Women have an emotional intelligence that men apparently do not have. We men, on the other hand, are emotionally impaired, and this somehow fuels our machismo. Simply stated, women handle their emotions better than we males. This "superiority" makes females dangerous in a sense—condemning and destructive when they want to be but very wise when motivated by good hearts. Kindness is the noblest fruit of intelligence. Solomon perceptively said,

> A good wife is the crown of her husband,
>   but she who brings shame is like rottenness in his bones (Proverbs 12:4).

Florencia never let go of my hand through that time of crisis, nor did I in her difficult moments.

How do we go about changing our history? How do we face down temptation? In Christ's wilderness temptations and in His victory are gathered together in a sense all the temptations and victories of humankind. This includes yours and mine. In the secret of His victory lies the secret to ours. In His forty-day ordeal, Jesus walked alone so that we might never have to feel alone.

Let's turn our eyes to that desert experience and behold the Savior of the world submitting His will to that of God the Father. Observe Him crying out to the Father and receiving the caring ministry of angels. We can appropriate His victory to our own lives.

In the desert

"And at the same time, if ever a real, thundering miracle was performed on earth, it was on that day, the day of those three temptations. . . . For in these three questions all of subsequent human history is as if brought together into a single whole and foretold; three images are revealed that will take in all the insoluble historical contradictions of human nature over all the earth."[3] This magnificent sentence was penned by the Russian writer Fyodor Dostoyevsky.

The Gospels narrate that before initiating His ministry, Jesus spent forty days fasting in the desert. In those circumstances, the devil appeared to test Him. There were three temptations by which Satan's diabolical skills were brought into play against man's three most vulnerable weaknesses.

What are these universal temptations that even today exercise great sway? What challenges do they imply? How can we overcome them? How did Christ gain the victory over them? The three temptations point to three specific issues in man's condition: appetite, presumption, and power.

Appetite

The Gospel account relates that "the tempter came and said to him, 'If you are the Son of God, command these stones to become loaves of bread' " (Matthew 4:3). Ellen White states, "Of all the lessons to be learned from our Lord's first great temptation none is more important than that bearing upon the control of the appetites and passions." She adds, "Through sensual *indulgence*, Satan seeks to blot from the soul every trace of likeness to God."[4]

The senses process sensations and stimuli from the environment; we pick these up by sight, hearing, smell, taste, and touch. (There is another "sense" that provides a degree of inner equilibrium; we call it common sense, which ironically, often ends up being the least common of the senses.) God gave us the senses to better enjoy life. The senses do not contaminate us. In a puritanical outlook, the senses are condemned in and of themselves; they are treated as if they were the root of perversity. We humans harbor within a kind of natural hatred against the inner forces that subject us. We hate what we fear most about ourselves and which we are least able to keep in check. And this repugnance is especially expressed in violent ways against sexual sins; these spring from our own impulses, and they terrify us: "The scribes and the Pharisees brought a woman who had been caught in adultery, and placing her in the midst they said to him, 'Teacher, this woman has been caught in the act of adultery. Now in the law Moses commanded us to stone such. What do you say about her?' " (John 8:3–5). The strength of the Christian message does not lie in pointing out the misery of man, but in highlighting the power of the Word to transform.

The problem is the indulgence of the senses as though these constituted the sole purpose in life. But don't be fooled:

the eye is not satisfied with seeing,
    nor the ear filled with hearing (Ecclesiastes 1:8).

Intemperance underlies the indulgence of the passions. The first temptation had to do with appetite—with the mouth. According to the Genesis story, Eve sinned when she ate the forbidden fruit.

The mouth is also the sounding board of our emotional afflictions: anorexia, bulimia, and obesity. These afflict hundreds of millions of people worldwide. By way of the mouth we not only satisfy our organic needs, responsible for physical sustenance, we likewise pursue addictive pleasures. The lyrics of a Latin tango that comes to mind belt out this line: *"Fumar es un placer sensual, cordial"* (Smoking is a warm, sensual pleasure). (But that doesn't tell the whole truth, does it?)

God's Word counsels us: "So, whether you eat or drink, or whatever you do, do all to the glory of God" (1 Corinthians 10:31). We need to learn from this text that the natural and supernatural are not totally distinct realms, far distant one from the other as in our limited thinking about heaven and earth. God is in my thoughts, but He is also in my body.

For this reason, the Bible teaches us to live in His presence not only through prayer, study of the Word, and meditation, but also by taking care of our bodies—what we eat and drink, and much more—so that the body becomes the temple of the Holy Spirit. To refrain from harmful food and drink, or other substances, is not an act of fanaticism. It is an expression of love toward oneself in gratitude for what God has given in this temple that is the human body. "Do you not know that you are God's temple and that God's Spirit dwells in you?" (1 Corinthians 3:16).

Judah Halevi, a Jewish poet and philosopher born in Spain in the eleventh century, wisely says, "Lord, where shall I find You? High and hidden is Your abode. And where shall I not find You if Your glory fills the world?" You and I are part of God's creation: the glory of God is expressed in our bodies. Your body and my body are the greatest manifestation of the glory of God on this earth. No engineering work is more sophisticated than the human body, and nothing is more beautiful.

But the indulgence of our senses does not necessarily start with the mouth, rather via the eyes and ears. The senses are deceptive. If you put a pencil in a glass of water, what you see is not its real image. The pencil has not become physically bent in that liquid. By their senses, people are lost. By indulging them, they are destroyed. Eve lifted the fruit to her mouth only after being seduced through her ears and eyes. She listened, she saw, and she ate.

The gorgeous figure of a woman can turn the poor weak head of a man crazy. Remember what came over David: "It happened, late one afternoon, when David arose from his couch and was walking upon the roof of the king's house, that he saw from the roof a woman bathing; and the woman was very beautiful. . . . So David sent messengers, and took her; and she came to him, and he lay with her. (Now she was purifying herself from her uncleanness.) Then she returned to her house" (2 Samuel 11:2, 5).

The story of David's sin is brief on salacious details, but the consequences of his act fatally affected the following generation. Lies and murder tainted his character: "In the morning David wrote a letter to Joab, and sent it by the hand of Uriah. In the letter he wrote, 'Set Uriah in the forefront of the hardest fighting, and then draw back from him, that he may be struck down, and die' " (verses 14, 15).

A woman's body penetrates a man's eyes, just like a man's words penetrate a woman's ears. The indulgence of the senses makes of men and women a "bite of bread" (see Proverbs 6:26). And thus homes and families are destroyed. The destiny of man is in a woman, and vice versa, but the truth about souls lies beyond the senses. It might start with the senses, but it doesn't end there. The most important relationship of human beings requires a solid foundation:

> Unless the LORD builds the house,
> those who build it labor in vain (Psalm 127:1).

Last weekend I went out to the fields to visit farm workers, to take them Bibles, and to pray with them. When I arrived at one of the harvesting fields that I had not visited for some time, the general supervisor indicated that he wanted to talk with me. I thought maybe he was going to tell me that I was a nuisance and they didn't want me coming around. But no, it was not that at all. He took the entire morning to escort me around to each of the work teams. Never had anyone in such a position given me so much time and assistance. When it came time for me to leave, the supervisor said, "Do you remember that I said I wanted to talk to you?"

"Yes, of course."

At the very moment when he began to lay out his thoughts, his cell phone rang. I could hear a lady's voice. He gave her a terse reply: "I'll call you back."

"Did you see that? That's what this is about. A woman is calling me. She flatters me with her words, and I like it. But I'm a married man."

"Well, if you are asking if I saw, I saw nothing. The one who saw was you," I responded.

"What do you mean?"

"That man is not so much tempted by the ears, but by his eyes. I am sure you saw her, you liked what you saw, and then you approached her and spoke with her. That's when you felt flattered by her words."

"How do you know that?"

"The devil knows more, not because he's the devil but because he's experienced." I wanted to break the tension a little with that comment.

I asked him how old he and his wife were: forty-seven and forty-six. And how old was this other woman? She had just turned thirty-seven. It really isn't necessary to say much more. He was desperate for this younger woman, who no doubt was prettier than his wife.

If you look up the word *flatter* in wise Solomon's Proverbs, you will find it referenced in the Wycliffe Bible, and you will find only a few texts that mention the word. If you look for references of the word *woman* in Ecclesiastes and

Proverbs, you will find numerous texts about virtuous women and many others about unsuspecting men getting caught in the traps of scheming women. Here is an example:

> For the lips of a loose woman drip honey,
>   and her speech is smoother than oil (Proverbs 5:3).

But let's put things in balance here. It is not just women who set the traps. For thousands of years, women have borne the stigma of being the first to fall into sin. They are portrayed as lurking about, trying to entrap poor, unsuspecting males. But my experience as a man and the father of two daughters has taught me other things. It is men who believe they have the right to subjugate and accost women. Machismo is a frightful thing. Men too often fail to realize how much harm we cause when we convert women into mere sex objects.

And this is what was happening with that supervisor. He liked what he saw, he felt flattered, and now he didn't know what to do. This same story happens time and again in every corner of the world: man feels he has a right to accost women.

Presumption

The temptation saga continues:

> Then the devil took him [Jesus] to the holy city, and set him on the pinnacle of the temple, and said to him, "If you are the Son of God, throw yourself down; for it is written,

> 'He will give his angels charge of you,'

and

> 'On their hands they will bear you up,
>   lest you strike your foot against a stone' " (Matthew 4:5, 6).

There is a danger that in place of faith we might substitute presumption, a trust in God through arrogance. As Umberto Eco says in his famous work *The Name of the Rose,* "the Devil is the arrogance of the spirit, faith without smile, truth that is never seized by doubt."[5] I have already said that reasonable doubt is always better than a presumptuous faith.

Presumption does not seek God but rather a miracle: "When Herod saw Jesus, he was very glad, for he had long desired to see him, because he had heard about

him, and he was hoping to see *some sign done by him*" (Luke 23:8; italics added).
Herod was a wicked man. He wasn't interested in the truth of God. Pride kept
faith from germinating in his heart. He would never give his life to Jesus. With
him, it was all about reaffirming his position and holding on to power. The
Teacher of Nazareth was insignificant to him. He just wanted entertainment—a
magic show—from the Nazarene, and Jesus knew it. He had already warned the
disciples: "Take heed, beware of the leaven of the Pharisees and the leaven of
Herod" (Mark 8:15). The leaven of the Pharisees and of Herod was presumption
born of selfishness and pride.

> As leaven, if left to complete its work, will cause corruption and decay, so
> does the self-seeking spirit, cherished, work the defilement and ruin of the
> soul.
>
> Among the followers of our Lord today, as of old, how widespread is this
> subtle, deceptive sin! How often our service to Christ, our communion
> with one another, is marred by the secret desire to exalt self! . . . To His
> own disciples the warning words of Christ are spoken: "Take heed and
> beware of the leaven of the Pharisees."
>
> . . . Only the power of God can banish self-seeking and hypocrisy.[6]

For the Argentine writer Leopoldo Lugones, "faith is a jagged mountain full of
precipices, and in its caves dwell the larvae of all vices."[7] The caverns and abysms
of faith are the deification and ostentation of an arrogant religiosity. Opposed to
that system, Jesus longed for the exercise of a free faith. He sought to promote in
men's souls dependence on God and not the manipulation of religious things or
their self-interested use. He sharply countered Satan: "Do not put the Lord your
God to the test" (Matthew 4:7, NIV). God is not at our beck and call; we cannot
use Him. The Spirit of God is sovereign: "The wind blows where it wills, and you
hear the sound of it, but you do not know whence it comes or whither it goes; so
it is with every one who is born of the Spirit" (John 3:8). We cannot steer God;
but if we humbly give ourselves to Him, He will guide us in the path of life.

Pride, which gives birth to presumption, is the great temptation of many religious leaders. This temptation is both subtle and powerful.

Power

"And the devil took him up, and showed him all the kingdoms of the world in
a moment of time, and said to him, 'To you I will give all this authority and their
glory; for it has been delivered to me, and I give it to whom I will. If you, then,
will worship me, it shall all be yours' " (Luke 4:5–7).

Satan offered Jesus authority and dominion over this world provided He recognized the devil's supremacy. It was the classical offer of power and empire, a temptation of power for power's sake. The problem is, the price is way too high; it requires sacrificing integrity, spurning the conscience, and taking a pass on honesty. But many do not mind paying the price; they are like ravenous wolves on the prowl, driven by a passion for power that trespasses all bounds and despises right values.

Michel Foucault, a French philosopher (1926–1984), said that strategy is the essence of power; that is to say, a set of maneuvers, tactics, techniques, and performances aimed at gaining supremacy. From Machiavelli's time, politicians have recognized that simulation underlies the exercise of power and that politics is less about territorial or state management and more about the art of deceptive posturing for the purposes of image. It is about scheming: a clever politician is a master at calculating his moves. He says what is convenient; he never says openly what he feels or thinks but only what is politically correct. For this reason, modern politicians have "bad press"; they are seen as the least reliable people in society.

However, not all people in political office seek power as an end in itself; some are true statesmen, dedicated to the service of the public. The key to overcoming corruption in the world is the spirit of service. Young Joseph is a fine biblical example of a God-fearing public servant: "And Pharaoh said to his servants, 'Can we find such a man as this, in whom is the Spirit of God?' . . . 'You shall be over my house, and all my people shall order themselves as you command' " (Genesis 41:38, 40).

But, it wasn't the political class who flocked to Jesus' side but rather the humble, honest folks. Pretense in the service of one's image is not just a problem typical of politicians; it is also common among those filling religious offices. For this reason, it is worth noting what Jesus said about this temptation for power: "You shall worship the Lord your God, and him only shall you serve" (Luke 4:8).

The worship of God is meant to safeguard us from the temptation of power. Created beings in His service are divinely fortified in the principles of humility, respect, mutual appreciation, and proper self-esteem. A consciousness of the divine trumps authoritarian and arrogant behavior; it favors altruism and solidarity. Jesus is no friend of ceremonious pretense and pontificating solemnity. A craving for the upper rungs of hierarchy is repugnant to the Master: "they love the place of honor at feasts and the best seats in the synagogues" (Matthew 23:6).

Today, twenty centuries after that day in the wilderness, the spirit of evil persists in its tantalizing operations, attacking us in the most vulnerable weak spots of our human nature. Those disquieting temptations continue drawing out our weaknesses—those that attempt to indulge our senses and snare us in presumption and power grasping.

Was human nature created capable of living above the senses and seeking the Bread of heaven? Was human nature created capable of not seeking miracles as the only reason for worshiping God? Was human nature created capable of not engaging in power struggles but instead of being faithful in freely seeking resolution with a humble heart?

Yes, humankind was created for all of this. But sin entered, intent on destroying the work of God. However, where Christ overcame, you and I can do the same. Nobody comes through temptation quite the same on the other side. If you are defeated, your ashes will be scattered into the air. But if you gain the victory in the name of God, you come forth as purified gold after going through a fire (1 Peter 1:6, 7). Focus your eyes on Jesus, the Victor in the wilderness.

FOR YOUR REFLECTION

1. What are the three ways that the devil seeks to destroy us?

2. Is pride the strongest temptation of religious people?

3. Can Christ empower us to overcome temptation? How so?

4. What does Psalm 51:1–5 mean to you?

1. George Eliot, *Romola,* chap. 9.

2. Matthew Henry, *The Comprehensive Commentary on the Holy Bible: Acts-Revelation,* 205.

3. Fyodor Dostoyevsky, *The Brothers Karamazov,* 252.

4. White, *The Desire of Ages,* p. 122; italics added.

5. Umberto Eco, *The Name of the Rose,* 477.

6. White, *The Desire of Ages,* 409.

7. Leopoldo Lugones, *Lunario sentimental.*

Chapter 8

Deliver Us From Evil

Destruction
The devil stirs at my side without ceasing;
There floats around me such an impalpable air;
I breathe it, feeling how my lungs burn
Filling them with an eternal desire and guilt.

Sometimes it takes, knowing my love of art,
The form of the most seductive woman,
And under special hypocritical pretenses
I accustom my tastes to nefarious pleasures.

That is how I carry on, far away from God's gaze,
Panting and broken by fatigue, to the center
Of the plains of tiring disgust, deep and deserted,

And tossed in my eyes, full of confusion,
Filthy garments, open wounds,
And the bloody dressings of destruction!
—Charles Baudelaire (French poet, 1821–1867)

Imaginary tags are what we use to categorize people. Nothing is easier than to attach a label, nor is anything less effective. This is because humans are as changeable as meandering rivers and as layered as onions. We believe that a label helps us find common ground with total strangers, or we somehow feel that we know them. It's as if these labels dispel the mystery behind all those people out there whom we conveniently package up as good or bad, fat or skinny, dumb or smart, black or white or in-between on the color scale. There are the normal people and the not-so-normal . . . the list is endless.

I'm sure if we had to label the house where wickedness resided in my child-hood neighborhood, it would have fallen on 1430 Peter Campbell Street. It was a home where migrants could stay while looking for jobs in the capital, and, of course, there was the occasional prostitute, and from time to time, a criminal on the lam would stay the night there. Lots of folks thereabouts were sure that the label of "evil" fit that location. Once I saw an elderly woman, who was in charge of bringing back any gossip, stop in front of the house and make the sign of the cross on herself. Wise Solomon said,

> The words of a gossip are like choice morsels;
>   they go down to a man's inmost parts (Proverbs 18:8, NIV).

I once read that the ability to speak several languages is a gift many people pos-sess, but the ability to keep one's mouth shut in any language is a gift precious few possess. The old woman in question did not have an off-switch for her mouth, especially regarding what went on behind those doors at 1430.

The main door facing the street of that Spanish-style building induced fear; it was black, with patches of paint that had flaked off, and it was a big, tall door, which, to my small stature as a kid, looked like the entrance to hell. However, I doubted that the house was the abode of the devil himself. From the people I saw coming and going, it seemed like a fascinating world to me, of people who came from very different walks of life and held very different standards. I confirmed this the first time I stepped through the door. I did so without my mother's permission, since she would always say, "Don't go near that house."

In front, there were seemingly endless white marble steps to climb just to get to the massive front door. I reached up and rang the bell for someone to open the security gate. The house was two stories tall, the tile floors were immacu-late. Two Carrara marble columns stood like sentinels watching over a bygone glory. A common courtyard served all the rooms on both floors; there was a little Andalusian-styled patio with geraniums in the garden. A classmate named Daniel lived there; he was my excuse for entering the house, and besides, we had a school assignment to work on.

The residents at 1430 were poor folks. Entire families crowded together in just one room; they had to share the bathroom with others. Nobody there had enough money to rent an apartment, but they were very supportive of each other and loyal. Most seemed to be honest, hardworking people with the same dreams as their better-off neighbors, whose checks didn't bounce. Almost all of them displayed an attitude of deference toward the rest of the neighborhood, as if they were at the lowest plane looking up. I wondered to myself whether that was humility or perhaps something else. Citizens of the capital always looked down on those from the interior parts of the country. They were called "canaries" (the "ignorant" people who had come from the Canary Islands, such as my grandfather). They were generally tagged as simpletons.

The second time I ventured into that house was to satisfy a not-too-innocent childish curiosity: I wanted to know what the rooms were like where the "women of the street" lived. I wondered about their lights, as I had heard they used colored bulbs. I had seen them entering in the morning and going out at night—after all, they were "ladies of the night." The outlandish way in which they were dressed made me laugh; they looked like they were wearing Halloween costumes. Daniel showed me where Betty and Gloria lived. I was surprised; their rooms were no different from all the others. Gloria had a husband and a son Enrique, whose father was not her current husband. Betty had only her son, Bobby. They were my schoolmates, and we later became friends.

I remember the look on the faces of those women. They would keep a wary eye out, like nervous creatures always on the alert. They avoided direct eye contact for the most part. Gloria was authoritarian and somewhat intolerant. Betty was more vulnerable and with a sweeter disposition, I would say, at least when speaking with me. They never made any solicitations to me or my friends, even after a few years when we were teenagers. I remember them as victims of their own choices rather than victimizers. Because it's one thing to do wrong, and it's another to suffer misery. The moral misery in which prostitutes live makes them dangers to themselves. They are victims of that vice. In time, they may change, but many cannot bear to live with their own history. Behind each one lies a tale of tears and broken childhood innocence.

When I gave myself to Christ, I went to visit Betty and share with her my testimony. She was no longer a woman of the night. Years had passed. She received me in her room at that same old address. She made us tea and sat attentively to hear what I had come to tell her. I opened the Bible and presented Jesus with all the innocence and strength of my first love. Betty let out a long sigh. She looked at me and said, "I am happy for you; you were able to do it." She hugged me, cried with emotion in my arms, and we prayed a long time on our knees. I never saw Betty again.

Jesus was labeled

For Jesus, it wasn't human weakness and human misery that were evil. That is precisely why He was accused of eating and associating with sinners. "And as he sat at table in the house, behold, many tax collectors and sinners came and sat down with Jesus and his disciples. And when the Pharisees saw this, they said to his disciples, 'Why does your teacher eat with tax collectors and sinners?' " (Matthew 9:10, 11).

Jesus' best friends were Lazarus, Martha, and Mary; the latter, "a woman of the night," saw Jesus as her personal Savior. Chapter 4 of the Gospel of John records a dialogue with another woman of the streets known as the Samaritan. John 8 recounts Jesus' encounter with the Magdalene woman. When the same religious leaders who had "lead their victim into sin," dragged her before the Master to trap Him and then stone the woman, Jesus began writing in the dust at their feet the sins those accusers had committed.[1] The Bible story continues as follows:

> He stood up and said to them, "Let him who is without sin among you be the first to throw a stone at her." And once more he bent down and wrote with his finger on the ground. But when they heard it, they went away, one by one, beginning with the eldest, and Jesus was left alone with the woman standing before him. Jesus looked up and said to her, "Woman, where are they? Has no one condemned you?" She said, "No one, Lord." And Jesus said, "Neither do I condemn you; go, and do not sin again" (John 8:7–11).

This is one of the most illuminating texts in the New Testament concerning the infinite understanding Jesus has of the human condition. He saw in human misery the consequences of evil in the world.

We believers like to quantify and qualify evil. It almost seems as if we bundle it up and then ascribe it to people, acts, concepts, and customs; in doing so that somehow distances it from us personally.

We feel more comfortable closing our eyes to our own failures and focusing on the shortcomings of others, and if we can exercise some control over those who don't do things like we think they should, and also toss in a dose of persecution, how good we then feel about ourselves! Misinterpreted, religion can become a horrendous medium of control and persecution. That certainly has been the case throughout human history. This is true in every religious community.

In Matthew 15, the profession of the Pharisees, the religious leaders of Jesus' time, is recorded, of putting the essence of evil into actions, rites, and traditions. The story reads as follows: "Then Pharisees and scribes came to Jesus from Jerusalem and said, 'Why do your disciples transgress the tradition of the elders? For they do not wash their hands when they eat' " (verses 1, 2).

Jesus did not remain silent about following the traditions of men to the detriment of what is good and right:

"You hypocrites! Well did Isaiah prophesy of you, when he said:

> 'This people honors me with their lips,
> but their heart is far from me;
> in vain do they worship me,
> teaching as doctrines the precepts of men.' "

And he called the people to him and said to them, "Hear and understand: not what goes into the mouth defiles a man, but what comes out of the mouth, this defiles a man" (verses 7–11).

To Jesus' way of thinking, evil is born in the heart and pours out from there to do its worst.

It is easier to identify the evil outside of us and reduce it to simplistic formulas. But that approach can lead us to commit great injustices, especially when done in the name of piety and God. That brings to mind the story of the pious old woman who threw slow-burning green wood onto the execution pyre for the Italian philosopher Giordano Bruno, accused by the church of heresy. Even in the name of piety we can produce suffering in the world.

The Pharisees wanted to get rid of Jesus, because according to them, He embodied evil. Matthew recorded proof of their intentions in chapter 12. It speaks for itself:

> At that time Jesus went through the grainfields on the Sabbath. His disciples were hungry and began to pick some heads of grain and eat them. When the Pharisees saw this, they said to him, "Look! Your disciples are doing what is unlawful on the Sabbath."
>
> He answered, "Haven't you read what David did when he and his companions were hungry? He entered the house of God, and he and his companions ate the consecrated bread—which was not lawful for them to do, but only for the priests. . . . If you had known what these words mean, 'I desire mercy, not sacrifice,' you would not have condemned the innocent. For the Son of Man is Lord of the Sabbath.". . .
>
> . . . [And] looking for a reason to accuse Jesus, they asked him, "Is it lawful to heal on the Sabbath?"
>
> He said to them, "If any of you has a sheep and it falls into a pit on the Sabbath, will you not take hold of it and lift it out? How much more valuable is a man than a sheep! Therefore it is lawful to do good on the Sabbath."

. . . [And] the Pharisees went out and plotted how they might kill Jesus (verses 1–14, NIV).

Back to my neighborhood

In the early years of the 1970s, a cloak of darkness began to settle over my neighborhood and the entire country. It could be seen approaching as clearly as a lightning storm brewing on the horizon.

It was a gray Friday morning announcing the arrival of winter. There wasn't even time to get out of bed to see whether the day had dawned cold and crisp when I heard machine-gun fire echoing behind the apartment. The firing came from the intersection of Rivera and Soca Avenues. There, on that morning of April 14, 1972, Subcommissioner Oscar Delgado and his chauffeur, Agent Carlos Leites, were gunned down by a squad of the left-wing urban guerrilla group known as the Tupamaros. A little while later, the former undersecretary of the Ministry of the Interior, Armando Acosta y Lara, and Lieutenant Commander Ernesto Motto were also assassinated. Just after noon, the police raided a house on Amazon Street and another on Perez Gomar Street. There were fatalities and arrests among the Tupamaro ranks. All hell seemed to be breaking loose. The fever of unrest rose rapidly, as in a patient in the throes of Ebola, but the truth is this was a virus that had been doing damage in society as a whole for years.

That armed conflict in the vicinity of my neighborhood was an echo of a much larger war in the Northern Hemisphere: the confrontation between the capitalist West and the communist East. In the south, blood was flowing down the streets to the river and staining the walls of the houses right there in my neighborhood. Caught in the crossfire, families found themselves separated by ideologies. Intolerance to the thoughts of one another was sowing the seeds of violence, and we could only expect more storms such as the prophet Hosea envisioned (Hosea 8:7). A long and infamous time of death and disappearances had befallen my country; it was to be its darkest time in national history. And just like in my neighborhood, the same was spreading throughout the country and throughout Latin America. Everyone seemed to be in arms against everyone else—rich against poor—without realizing that it would only end in misery for all.

By then, I had come of age. Like many other youth, I tried to remain a passive observer in a war that had its origin in foreign interests. But I knew that eventually I would have to make my decision and commit to the fight. We were a generation under tremendous pressure to take a stand, but it wasn't clear, at least to me, whether I should enter into the fight. Many young people were recruited for both sides, either with the guerrillas or with the army. Many of my friends would be facing these challenges for the rest of their lives and into the next generation. Even today, as I write these lines forty years later, there are old wounds that have never healed.

At last, I reached my decision. In the moment of greatest darkness in my life, when the world was crashing down around me, when letters from both sides were arriving at our apartment urging me to join their ranks, a young Spanish pastor, Luis Perez, from Toledo, taught me by word and example about the Christ I had not really known before. Mere months before Uruguay fell under a military dictatorship, in June 1973, I was on my way abroad to study theology and prepare to serve as a pastor. God definitely had other plans for my life.

It is a fearful thing when the power of evil comes disguised as ideology and intolerance, because radicalized human beings are capable of killing for what they believe. A sane, balanced person is capable of recognizing that he might be wrong; apologies can be offered for mistakes made. But fanatics who are convinced they have the truth are caught in a trap of ignorance and do not grow. Becoming intolerant of others is just a step short of taking lives.

There are invisible forces that propel us to think and act in certain ways. Evil begins its trajectory in the mind of each person. Personal sin moves on to become public sin. What began as just an idea finally evolves into a tragedy. This is the history of humankind—largely, that comes down to a long history of wars. The twentieth century left hundreds of millions of people dead, victims of conflicting ideologies. Two world wars brutalized and traumatized nations on a scale never before seen. Anonymous cemeteries in concentration camps and gulags are full of the unfortunate fallen. This new century opened with so-called civilized wars, which are actually waged over economic and political interests. Weapons are becoming ever more lethal—chemical, biological, nuclear. Man has become a wolf to his fellow man.

True peace among nations will be possible only when there is real peace in the hearts of the individual people. This is Jesus' promise: "Peace I leave with you; my peace I give to you; not as the world gives do I give to you. Let not your hearts be troubled, neither let them be afraid" (John 14:27).

Cosmic conflict

That armed conflict that took place in my country was the expression of the Cold War, yet no less cruel, between capitalism and communism. There is, however, a cosmic conflict that is the mother of all wars here on earth. It is the conflict between good and evil. Evil is not an act or a human person; it cannot be exhausted by a stream of words, nor can it be prevented with rituals. Evil is a power superior to man. "For we are not contending against flesh and blood, but against the principalities, against the powers, against the world rulers of this present darkness, against the spiritual hosts of wickedness in the heavenly places," says Paul in Ephesians 6:12. This is the cosmic context of all our human conflicts.

In the prophetic texts of the Old Testament (Ezekiel 28:14–19; Isaiah 14:12–14), the origin of evil is presented: Lucifer, an exalted celestial being, fell under an insatiable ambition for power. Created perfect, wise, and very beautiful, with special privileges because of his high rank in the heavenly courts, he was the "covering cherub," the highest authority among angelic beings. But, incomprehensibly, his character became degraded as a result of his ambition for supremacy.

> "You were blameless in your ways
>   from the day you were created,
>   till iniquity was found in you" (Ezekiel 28:15).

He determined,

> "I will ascend to heaven;
> above the stars of God
>   I will set my throne on high;
> I will sit on the mount of assembly
>   in the far north;
> I will ascend above the heights of the clouds,
>   I will make myself like the Most High" (Isaiah 14:13, 14).

Because he persisted in pride, Lucifer was finally expelled from heaven, becoming Satan, who incites humans to do wrong and who promotes what was the object of his own fall.

War began in heaven with the devil. In the course of time, it spread to the newly created earth. The fall of man inaugurated the permanent presence of evil in this world (Genesis 3).

The presence of evil

The Bible speaks of the emergence of evil, but it does not explain evil, because evil is inexplicable. The Bible cannot explain how sin originated in the heart of Lucifer. Because if it could be explained, it could be justified. But evil has no justification. Man is responsible for his actions, and guilt rests upon him if he lets evil dwell in his heart. Our human family also suffers from the side effects of a war fought in heaven even before our planet was created. Consequently, man is also a victim and therefore worthy of mercy. That is why "God sent the Son into the world, not to condemn the world, but that the world might be saved through him" (John 3:17).

The question of evil has perturbed the minds of philosophers and theologians throughout history. Its presence in the world raises a question that calls for a solution. That's why philosophy and theology have given it so much attention on a wide front. Evil does not pose a problem as if it were a matter of a mathematical calculation, which reasoning resolves—such as finding the square root of a number. Evil presents a *question*. Not simply a solvable problem. A question that has no explanation, but it does have an end.

While evil is inexplicable, nevertheless, we can face it and recognize it. The underlying question regarding the presence of evil in the world has to do with suffering. In this matter the German philosopher Friedrich Nietzsche makes sense: for modern man, you and me, the question is not so much suffering as the lack of an answer to the question of why we suffer.

This question has also been addressed by *theodicy*, a branch of rational theology, also called natural theology, and by philosophy. But there is no answer. In their efforts to defend God in the presence of evil in the world, theologians have tried many theories. From Saint Augustine to Saint Thomas, theologians have tended toward the doctrine of crime and punishment. That is, there is suffering because of some failure or fault. In other words, if someone suffers, it is because that person deserves it. If he is not the direct cause for the suffering, it could be blamed on his ancestors. Jesus faced this theology squarely: "And his disciples asked him, 'Rabbi, who sinned, this man or his parents, that he was born blind?' Jesus answered, 'It was not that this man sinned, or his parents, but that the works of God might be made manifest in him' " (John 9:2, 3). Suffering is not explained, but it is cited as the condition by which the glory of God is revealed. This question is central to the book of Job. The German philosopher Immanuel Kant echoes the lament of Job: I pray that my faults and misfortunes are put into the balance (see Job 6:2; 31:6). Kant considered hypocritical and untruthful the notion that to justify or explain suffering, it is necessary to find some fault.

This is what my mother-in-law felt in her final hours. She didn't suffer so much from physical causes as she did from the notion that God was sending her suffering because of her past sins. "I asked God's forgiveness for all the bad things I did, but now I continue to suffer." It was not easy to get that idea out of her dear old head. The idea too readily morphs from the proposition *man sins, then suffers*, to *man sins, therefore he suffers*. My mother-in-law was a religious woman, a very good person, but no amount of personal suffering would have redeemed her. It is exclusively the suffering Christ endured that offers us redemption.

Christ suffered and died for all humankind, for you and for me as well. All that remains is for us to thank Him for His sacrifice, not to try to add in our own portion of suffering. I comforted my mother-in-law with these words: "God loves you infinitely more than I do. I wouldn't let you suffer. Much less He." And I read her this text: "But when Christ had offered for all time a single sacrifice for sins, he sat down at the right hand of God. . . . Where there is forgiveness of these, there is no longer any offering for sin" (Hebrews 10:12, 18). My mother-in-law was suffering the collateral consequences of living in a fallen world, but she most certainly was not suffering in payment for her sins. Christ suffered and paid the price of sin for all of us who turn to Him. Hers were long ago confessed and blotted out. Now she could gratefully rest in peace.

In this world, the tension between guilt and punishment is never fully relieved nor resolved. Look, for example, at the guilty murderer who is condemned to death for his crime. Does his execution restore to life the victim so cruelly deprived of ongoing years and loving relationships? Clearly, it does not. What we are left with is a death penalty that looks more like simple vengeance than restorative or rectifying punishment. But that is our reality in a fallen world, and we can do little more about it than make societal improvements this side of that better world to come.

This relationship between fault and suffering, between crime and punishment, has a counterpart in another no less inadequate idea: that we can produce merits and that these in turn are deserving of rewards. In other words, if we make certain sacrifices, we can expect rewards. Thus, religion becomes an effort to accumulate merits for salvation—a kind of temple tax that lets us into heaven. Jesus said, "Go and learn what this means, 'I desire mercy, and not sacrifice.' For I came not to call the righteous, but sinners" (Matthew 9:13). Salvation is manifested in a transformation, not in a summation of works. And repentance is not shown with tears but with changes. The world changes by your example, not by your opinion. Not with words or tears. Not with intentions but with actions—the smallest action is better than the greatest intention.

This thought that the world does not change by tears brings to mind a poem by Charles Baudelaire, an admired French poet:

> Our sins are stubborn, our repentance faint,
> We sell our weak confessions at high price,
> Returning gaily to the bogs of vice,
> Thinking base tears can cleanse our every taint.[2]

These lines are magnificent. Profoundly sincere. With sensibility and consciousness of his own evil, the poet brings out in these lines an antithetical parallel: something that should go in a certain direction goes in the opposite direction. The more aware of our own evil we are, the more we should repent. Our acts of repentance should be real and more intense, so that our capacity to sin is thereby weakened. But what happens is just the opposite: our sins are "hardheaded," stubborn; we insist on sinning, and consequently our repentance grows weaker and weaker. We believe that confessing our sins is enough to pay our debt, our guilt. But that isn't so, because our repentance is weak, our cry is ignoble. We suffer, we cry a little, but we do not change. We just cry for a spell so that we will feel better about ourselves. Oh, what harm has resulted from the establishment of the confessional! We sin, we confess, we purge, and we feel better—ready to go out and do it all over again. This is what the poem means when it says we return "gaily to the bogs of vice."

Man has a fascination for constantly returning to the filth of sin. This is the metaphysical ambiguity of evil and of sin that fascinates and seduces us. The poet David states it clearly:

> Behold, I was brought forth in iniquity,
>   and in sin did my mother conceive me (Psalm 51:5).

And Jesus says, "Watch and pray, that you may not enter into temptation; the spirit indeed is willing, but the flesh is weak" (Matthew 26:41). Our repentance is weak because we love sin. In a sense, sin is linked to an act of love. The Greek word *agapē* is used both to refer to that special type of God's love, which is the core of the New Testament, and to signify love for sin. In Luke 11:43, Jesus condemned the Pharisees because they loved (*agapaó*) occupying the best seats in the synagogue. Similarly, 2 Timothy 4:10 tells us that Demas abandoned the Christian way when he "fell in love" (*agapaó*) with this present world. Sin is a love that is centered on the wrong object. It is a sick love.

Life is like an egg: if you break it from the outside, its life ends; but if it cracks open from the inside by an interior force, a new life begins. The big changes in your life begin from the inside and then manifest themselves outwardly. The work of salvation generating this kind of transformation is of absolute divine origin. The dead have nothing to offer, nor can they do anything to have life: "And you he made alive, when you were dead through the trespasses and sins" (Ephesians 2:1).

Of course, the good works that arise from a transformed life are in the purview of God. Paul approves of "faith working through love" (Galatians 5:6). He congratulates the Thessalonians for "your work of faith and labor of love" (1 Thessalonians 1:3). And part of his work was to call the Gentiles to the "obedience of faith" (Romans 1:5; 16:26). These works in time would be rewarded: "Your Father who sees in secret will reward you" (Matthew 6:4). God is just. In contrast to that, there is this noxious idea that allows for self-promotion in spiritual matters—do good works in order to reap personal rewards. This notion produces church members who are proud of their own achievements. They are the sort who feel called to spy on their fellow members. They assume the role of judge. But out of their poor judgment springs ill will and envy; they become incensed when they see someone receive a blessing that they feel is undeserved. This is a reason why many young people do not come to Christ. In my own case, it took me some years to surrender to Jesus; partly because of my own rebellion, and partly because some believers seemed to be fools or perverse. Eventually, the love of Christ put things right in my heart.

Once again: The Bible speaks of the emergence of evil, but it cannot explain how it originated. If it can be explained, it can be justified. Yet evil cannot be justified. We cannot understand how in a perfect universe with a loving God, evil could have arisen.

You may say that our faults are paid in this world, our own and those of others. But it is not so: "There is a vanity which takes place on earth, that there are righteous men to whom it happens according to the deeds of the wicked, and there are wicked men to whom it happens according to the deeds of the righteous. I said that this also is vanity" (Ecclesiastes 8:14).

What can we do?

So then, in the presence of evil shall we keep silent just because we can't explain its existence?

Should we submit to resignation in the face of its power? No, never! Otherwise evil will triumph. When, in silence, we look the other way or we pretend to be distracted in the face of injustice, then we increase the quota of evil in the world and we kill a hope for a better world. The presence of evil calls for a counterstrike and is the occasion for the glory of God to be revealed through our actions. Paul exhorted, "Do not be overcome by evil, but overcome evil with good" (Romans 12:21). The answer to evil is good. But evil is not overthrown merely by words; it requires deeds. If religion has lost power in this world, it is largely because its ethical content has drained away. It has become a symbolical emptiness for modern men and women. But you and I, even by our small-scale actions, can increase good in the world. This should be our commitment day by day and as often as the opportunity arises. It should also be the guiding light for politicians: to enact laws that are fair and beneficial to the disadvantaged.

I just read in an American newspaper an encouraging article concerning my homeland. Uruguay has taken in fifty Syrian families rescued from the clutches of civil war. And more families will follow them in the near future. Photographs showed the faces of those men, women, and children who, through diplomatic efforts, were able to depart that war-torn land. Their haggard faces reveal some of the pain and suffering they have been through. There were a few brave smiles for the cameras. Among the contingent were two pregnant young women carrying the next generation soon to be born in a democratic, peaceful country with abundant food. In response to certain voices opposed to this act of humanitarian hospitality, the president of my country said, "We cannot stop a cruel and unjust war being waged far away, but we can carry out small acts that minimize the evil."

Those who have it the worst in this world are present so that "the works of God might be made manifest" in them (John 9:3). Countries and their societies do not become great simply because of their favorable geography or their expanding gross national products but because of their spirit of generosity.

Engraved on a bronze plaque and mounted inside the lower level of the pedestal of the Statue of Liberty in New York is a poem by Emma Lazarus. The last part says,

> "Keep, ancient lands, your storied pomp!" cries she
> With silent lips. "Give me your tired, your poor,
> Your huddled masses yearning to breathe free,
> The wretched refuse of your teeming shore.
> Send these, the homeless, tempest-tost to me,
> I lift my lamp beside the golden door!"

God is an eternal beacon of light for the hungry, the outcast, the homeless, the sinners, and the hopeless. He works miracles on their behalf.

Deliver us from evil

What does the statement "Deliver us from evil" mean? This petition of Christ finds in Christ Himself the answer to the question: "The reason the Son of God appeared was to destroy the works of the devil" (1 John 3:8). Evil is dual: there is an evil that is committed, and there is an evil that is suffered. There is an evil committed by the victimizer, and there are the effects of evil suffered by the victim. The evil you and I commit is intended for others, and even at ourselves, because there are times when we are our own worst enemies. The Word of God tells us that for this evil that we ourselves commit, there is forgiveness. And for the evil we suffer, there exists hope.

Forgiveness and hope are the only answers for evil. If this were not so, how could we otherwise understand the human propensity to seek revenge on the one hand, or to sink into despair on the other? Revenge and despair—the counterparts to forgiveness and hope—are all that exists with which to face the irreparable nature of evil.

But forgiveness and hope come to span the gap that exists in human justice. By that, I mean the gap that exists between the offense and the punishment. If you have suffered an irreparable wrong, all that remains is forgiveness, because human justice can never fully repair the wrong even if it tried. This does not mean that we deny law its due process or that we make no effort to seek proper redress for damage done to the innocent.

It means only that human justice is poor and defective and that forgiveness and hope belong to a superior justice.

In the Cross, there is power to confront evil. "I have been crucified with Christ; it is no longer I who live, but Christ who lives in me; and the life I now live in the flesh I live by faith in the Son of God, who loved me and gave himself for me" (Galatians 2:20). "I can do everything through Christ who strengthens me" (Philippians 4:13, GW).

Forgiveness is God's answer to your sin and mine, to the damage you and I inflict on others and on ourselves. We give and we receive. Hope is the gift that bridges the gap between your present and your future. If you have taken steps towards reconciliation with your brother and have pardoned his offenses, there is room to hope he will reconsider and seek reconciliation too. Patient waiting is an important part. He is your fellow man, your brother, part of your life, and deserves that consideration. But if the other does not respond, your forgiveness redeems you, and hope remains. Patience is born of hope; it is of a bitter root, but it produces sweet fruit.

Hope always remains because it is the last to go. There is a story about three fishermen who gathered at a favorite spot at Arroyo Maldonado in my country. They hadn't caught anything for several years, but that didn't stop them from getting together every Sunday to bait their hooks and toss their lines into the water.

But there is an even deeper dimension to hope—the hope of eternal life. The wages of sin is death, but "God so loved the world that he gave his only Son, that whoever believes in him should not perish but have eternal life" (John 3:16).

There is an eternal sense in this present life. If you feel yourself getting older, if day by day you are more aware of the certainty of your own mortality, if you are suffering the loss of a loved one, Jesus' petition, "Deliver us from evil" becomes the blessed hope of the second coming of Christ. In the next chapter, we will discuss further this blessed hope.

FOR YOUR REFLECTION

1. Is human misery an evil in itself?

2. What was the label that Jesus received?

3. What did the Sabbath mean for Jesus? Read Matthew 12:1–13.

4. Does evil receive its justice in this world?

---

1. White, *The Desire of Ages,* 461.
2. Charles Baudelaire, "To the Reader," in *Flowers of Evil.*

Chapter 9

For Thine Is the Kingdom, and the Power, and the Glory

Sower of Fruit
You left in silence
Nocturnal
In the most delicate way
So as not to disturb

On tiptoe
Barefoot of blame
Lightly burdened
Free of negotiations
Just small hypocrisies
And great betrayals

Naked of arrogance
Clothed in innocence
Humble
Peasant
Generous

But you did not go far
Today I saw you among the peach trees
Red with springtime
And the jasmine produced
Scents of your memory so white

Today I remembered the vine
Sweet shadow of February
And I summoned the blue eyes
Of your firstborn

So I dare say
That memory brings you
Perhaps closer
And frees your word
In a way
That is more effective
And much warmer

We are debtors
To your faith
To your hope

And also I dare say
That from so much believing
And so much sowing
You have converted into a debtor
The One in whom you knew
To wait for.

—Ricardo Bentancur

Rudy was Mima's boyfriend, the rebellious daughter of Papa Flores. She had found a boyfriend who could measure up to her expectations: the perfect atheist. Rudy was the son of an Italian family, a math teacher, and foulmouthed, particularly ironic when heaping insults on sacred things. I remember evenings together with them at the Flores home when Rudy and Pocho, Papa Flores's son, would really get into it with strong words and arguments. Pocho was studying theology and preparing to be a minister. Those discussions generally ended abruptly with Pocho trying his best to remain patient, an essential quality for one planning on a pastoral vocation. Rudy, on the other hand, would leave the living room reeling from his motormouthed blasphemies of every degree and color. I never heard from other lips blasphemies of quite that caliber. Sometimes it made me wince from guilty embarrassment, but I have to admit, some of his blasts were so original that they made me laugh in spite of myself.

Of course, then I felt all the more chagrined. Later, I would relate it all to my mother and she would respond, "Those Italians are always so irreverent." If that was so, then Rudy Vadagnini was no exception. We all knew that with him we couldn't talk religion. His thing was math; I remember when he helped me prepare for a sophomore high school exam in algebra and trigonometry. Rudy was generous with his time and knowledge; he didn't mince words while helping me study. He drove me on with insults, but that was just the way his mouth worked. He had a brilliant mind and a warm, generous heart, like so many Italians. I passed the exam; all I know of math I owe to Rudy.

Some years passed, and I accepted Jesus Christ. One evening I went to visit Rudy and Mima; they had married and had two children. I wanted to give them my testimony of faith. They looked at me as if an alien from outer space were standing there in front of them. Puzzled, they changed the subject and invited me to have dinner with them. Later, when it was time to go, I told them that I wanted to be a pastor. "Don't be a schmuck! Use your intelligence for something else. You'll starve to death!" That night I prayed for Rudy and Mima.

More years passed, and we went our separate ways, but I never stopped thinking of and praying for the Vadagnini family. There are people who are far away in time and space, but they always remain close to the heart on a daily basis. Some friends are closer than brothers of the same blood; they are the threads of life and community that we tie into for all time. They are the "family" we elect rather than inherit, and we love them all the same. It is that mutual affection that will lift the spirit time and again, even when years roll by and geography gets in between.

Jesus spoke about the greatest dimension of love toward one's friends: "Greater love has no man than this, that a man lay down his life for his friends" (John 15:13).

Early in October 2014 I received a call from Mima. Her voice echoed over the phone just like I remembered it from my childhood memories of Campbell Street. It was uncanny, and I felt transported back as if the years had never passed. Though now in her senior years, her voice was lively, vibrant like long ago. She commented about the Facebook page of her younger daughter, with whom she is now living; there was a photo of her granddaughter she wanted me to see—a beautiful fifteen-year-old who is the family joy. And then she told me what her reason was for making the call: "I wanted to tell you that some years ago I accepted Christ as my Savior, was baptized, and now go to church. Finally, the seed planted by my mother bore fruit . . . late but certain. Better late than never, ha!" Mima, the rebellious one in her family; I remember those years when her mother prayed and wept for her.

"That's wonderful, I congratulate you. The emotion of hearing from you leaves me speechless. Give me a few seconds to let my mind process this moment and your news. It's been so many years!" Then I asked about Rudy.

"He bit the dust a few years ago," she said. Typical Mima, she had never been dignified or ceremonious. And this time was no exception even when referring to the death of her life partner, who had suffered a fatal heart attack. I was silent. I was struggling to absorb the fact. "Bit the dust." The words kept repeating in my mind. And then she continued: "But I also have more good news. Rudy accepted Jesus some years before he died; it was the best thing that happened to us late in life."

I kept silent for a long moment. I wanted to savor those words, but tears were welling up and ready to roll down my cheeks. I didn't want to break down crying, so taking a long breath I composed myself so I could speak normally.

"Tell me more."

Then Mima recounted the following: "Once I started going to church, I said to myself: *I'll convert this hardheaded atheist.* So one cold winter night we went to bed early and I asked him, 'Would you like to read the Proverbs with me?' Well, he didn't say Yes or No. So I started to read some of the Proverbs to him. Months passed and one night, to my surprise, Rudy asked to borrow my Bible. I lent it to him and could never get it back. It was the only Bible we had, so I finally had to go buy myself another one."

"And what book of the Bible did Rudy like the most?" I asked.

"The Gospel of John. That's where he really discovered Jesus and grew to love Him forever. The grace of Christ overcame him. Today I await the second coming of Christ so I can see Rudy again."

The cross and the second coming of Christ

All believers await the second coming of Christ because we know that "the kingdom, and the power, and the glory" are all about Him (Matthew 6:13, KJV). That's what the Bible says: "The kingdom of the world has become the kingdom of our Lord and of his Christ, and he shall reign for ever and ever" (Revelation 11:15).

The Second Advent is closely linked with the first coming of Christ. If Christ had not come the first time and had not achieved a decisive victory over sin (Colossians 2:15), we would have no reason to believe He will return to finish His redemptive work. But because we have evidence that "he has appeared once for all at the end of the age to put away sin by the sacrifice of himself," we have reason to believe that He "will appear a second time, not to deal with sin but to save those who are eagerly waiting for him" (Hebrews 9:26, 28).

The Cross gives meaning to the expectation of Christ's second coming. When the Lord was hanging on the cross, the promise that He made to the thief beside Him offers assurance to every one of us (Luke 23:42, 43), especially to those who believe. The cross of Christ stands out sharply against the backdrop of history. It is not time that gives relevance to the Cross, but the Cross that gives relevance to time and to the life of man. To accept the prophetic truth concerning the second coming of Christ from the perspective of the Cross gives meaning and certainty to our lives and answers the deepest pondering of humankind: Is this mortal life all that we can expect? In a hopeful sense, it also answers the cry of the desperately lonely child from Managua.

In essence, the second coming of Christ constitutes the epicenter of all theology, according to the theologian Jürgen Moltmann. For it responds to the question of death and clarifies the nature and the state of the dead. Concerning that, the apostle Paul says, "But we would not have you ignorant, brethren, concerning those who are asleep, that you may not grieve as others do who have no hope. For since we believe that Jesus died and rose again, even so, through Jesus, God will bring with him those who have fallen asleep" (1 Thessalonians 4:13, 14). In other words, Christ will not only come for the living but also for the dead.

But how can that be? Haven't we always heard that when man dies he goes either to heaven or to hell? (Lately, it seems like purgatory has been removed from reference.) The doctrine of the second coming of Christ clarifies precisely this point: man is a mortal being. He doesn't continue living after he dies.

The mortal soul

The Bible says that God "formed man of dust from the ground, and breathed into his nostrils the breath of life; and man became a living being" (Genesis 2:7). So, we are stardust—made with the material of the universe. It sounds poetic. But we are no more than dust and time. Our genealogy begins and ends on the earth. Not much to be proud of.

The Hebrew term *nephesh chayyah,* in Genesis 2:7, is translated as "living being" or "living soul." It isn't designated just for human beings; it also applies to marine animals, insects, reptiles, and beasts—to all living things (Genesis 1:20, 24; 2:19). The Bible says man became "a living soul" (Genesis 2:7, KJV). Nothing in the story of Creation indicates that man received a soul, that is, some kind of separate entity that was united to his human body at Creation.

The Hebrew word *nephesh,* translated as "soul," denotes individuality or personality; meanwhile, the Old Testament Hebrew word *ruach,* translated "spirit," refers to the essential spark of life in human existence. It describes the divine energy or vital principle that animates humans and all living things. Psalm 146:4 says that when man dies, the breath (*ruach*) leaves the body. "The dust returns to the earth as it was, and the spirit [*ruach*] returns to God who gave it" (Ecclesiastes 12:7; compare Job 34:14, 15). In the Bible, neither *nephesh* nor *ruach* denote an intelligent entity capable of separate existence apart from the physical body. So, from that, we see that when man dies, he ceases to exist. He goes nowhere.

Obviously, if the soul was immortal, if man passed to the "great beyond" without experiencing death, then the return of Christ and the resurrection would make little sense. It would suffice for God to move directly to the judgment once the physical body of the individual had died, gone to heaven, gone to hell, or wherever. But hope in the second coming of Christ tells us that man is mortal, and that is why it is necessary for the Son of God to return to the earth to complete His work of redemption. He comes this time not to free us from the power of sin but from the presence of evil. This is when the final plea in the Lord's Prayer is fulfilled: "Deliver us from evil."

The question concerning death is very serious indeed. Faith doesn't lift any weight off the matter; presumption, on the other hand, does. Some believe that ritualistically repeating the Lord's Prayer a few times and carrying out a few good deeds on earth will earn them a nice little place in heaven. But it just isn't so. Death brings a close to each and every one of man's senses in this world. Unless we take a good hard look at the seriousness of death, we won't be able to correctly value what God plans for us beyond this present world.

We cannot properly value the work of Christ or comprehend the value of life in all its magnitude if we do not grasp the reality of death as taught in the Bible. Too often the faith of Christians is like a compliant sentiment that digests what others have chewed up for us.

Confusing faith with doctrine is like confusing digestion with anatomy. I might know a lot about anatomy but still digest food poorly. True faith is learned in life, not in catechisms. In the consciousness of death, we love. This is because love is the impulse of life against death. In the face of the anguish of nothingness, faith is born. Faith is the blessed gift of God given to the courageous, to those who do not conform to this world, nor to the "brewer's widow." Nothing could be further from the truth than the thought sustained by existentialist philosophers, such as Sartre and his disciples. They see in nothingness both the origin and the final purpose of man, and therefore put a notion to the weariness of life—a weariness of modern man that is born when he conforms himself with the "brewer's widow," because he does not allow himself to have faith.

"Death is swallowed up in victory."
"O death, where is thy victory?
O death, where is thy sting?"

exclaims Paul triumphantly (1 Corinthians 15:55).

The basis of this hope

Nietzsche said that hope "is, in truth, the greatest of evils for it lengthens the ordeal of man."[1] Of course, there is always a pinch of wisdom in a skeptical view of life. Nietzsche was a pessimist; or rather an optimist regarding the strengths of man, though not those of God. Contrary to Nietzsche, we can say that hope is the greatest of evils when it is founded on the possibilities of man. But it is blessed when founded on God. That is the difference.

Paul says, "So when God desired to show more convincingly to the heirs of the promise the unchangeable character of his purpose, he interposed with an oath, so . . . we . . . might have *strong encouragement* to seize the hope set before us" (Hebrews 6:17, 18; italics added). You and I have a hope that is guaranteed by the Eternal One.

The certainty of the Second Coming is rooted in the reliability of the Word of God. Shortly before His death, Jesus told His disciples that He would return to His Father to prepare a place for them. And He promised to "come again" (John 14:3). Just as the first coming of Christ was announced to world in the Old Testament, so His second coming is also predicted in all the Scriptures. Even before the Flood, God revealed to Enoch that the second coming of Christ would put an end to sin, suffering, and death. The patriarch prophesied, "Behold, the Lord came with his holy myriads, to execute judgment" (Jude 14, 15).

A thousand years before Christ, the psalmist spoke of the second coming of the Lord to gather His people:

> Our God comes, he does not keep silence,
> > before him is a devouring fire,
> > round about him a mighty tempest.
> He calls to the heavens above
> > and to the earth, that he may judge his people (Psalm 50:3, 4).

Christ's disciples rejoiced in the promise of His return. In the midst of all the difficulties they experienced, the sensation of security produced by this promise never failed to renew their courage and strength. Their Master would return and take them to His Father's house (John 14:1–3)!

Conclusion

It was not until my father-in-law died that I fully understood the truth about Christ's second coming. Hours before his death, which he saw approaching, he underlined in his Bible every text that referred to the second coming of Christ (such as 1 Corinthians 15:51–55; Malachi 4:1–3; 2 Peter 3:10–13). We had gone to visit him that weekend before he died. He was healthy and strong at eighty-four years old and still working hard at home. That Sunday afternoon when we said Goodbye, he looked at me, through his blue eyes, with that serene paternal look and said, "It is possible that I won't see you again here, but up there we will see each other again." Pointing towards heaven, he indicated where his hopes were centered. He sensed that his departure was near. At that moment, I had the irrevocable conviction that he had been the father I had never had. I loved him as a father, and he said Goodbye to me as to a beloved son, realizing he would not see me again in this life. After his death, I composed the verses that appear as the introduction to this chapter. I am convinced that his departure is not final. He spent his time on earth in the blessed hope. If he had focused only on the present reality, his faith would have been in vain, because he died without seeing the Lord descending in glory. But because Jesus gave him a sense of his time, he knew how to go to rest in the Eternal One, anchoring his faith beyond this earthbound time. Thus, he died with the assurance of seeing Jesus face-to-face. He loved this text: "Men of Galilee, why do you stand looking into heaven? This Jesus, who was taken up from you into heaven, will come in the same way as you saw him go into heaven" (Acts 1:11). The angels declared that the same Lord who had just departed heavenward—a personal being of flesh and bone, not a spiritual entity (Luke 24:36–43)—would return to this world. His second coming would be as literal and personal as His ascension. It wouldn't be simply an inner experience, or invisible, but rather a very real encounter with a visible Person. My father-in-law wanted to see Jesus face-to-face, because the coming of the Lord will be visible to every human eye, as Revelation 1:7 says. My father-in-law had the innocence of a child.

In this age of reason, perhaps believers have an unsustainable ingenuousness, of which those who do not believe (the gentlemen of resignation) make fun (2 Peter 3:4). But the gentlemen of faith believe against all logic, because they possess the dignity of the innocent.

My father-in-law *kept watch*. He knew his Master's counsel: "Watch therefore, for ye know neither the day nor the hour wherein the Son of man cometh" (Matthew 25:13, KJV). He saw the signs of the coming of Jesus, which indicated that it would be soon (Matthew 24); he longed for the coming of his Lord; but fundamentally, he kept watch. To keep watch means to fight to stay awake, to battle the sleep of resignation. "Life is a dream," Pedro Calderón said.

It is the sleep into which all mortals fall, like that into which the ten virgins in Matthew 25 fell. We all live alienated at times from our Lord, but there will be moments in which the Lord will come into our lives to wake us up from our sleep. When that moment comes upon you, arise and keep watch. The poet

Antonio Machado expresses the idea beautifully:

> I love Jesus, who said to us:
> Heaven and earth will pass away.
> When heaven and earth have passed away,
> my word will remain.
> What was your word, Jesus?
> Love? Affection? Forgiveness?
> All your words were
> one word: Wakeup.[2]

If you have honored my words by accompanying me to the end of this testimonial, then somehow I feel responsible for what this book might have produced in your heart. Martin Luther King Jr. once said, "If I helped someone to have hope, I will not have lived in vain." Just one person is enough because in that one is found all humanity. We are a drop in the ocean, but the whole ocean is contained in that drop. If my words have helped you, then this book was not written in vain.

Neither you nor I nor anyone else is completely free. Neither you nor I nor anyone else can reach absolute happiness. Neither you nor I nor anyone else has the absolute truth. The words I have written in this book are intended to be a testimony, not dogmatic words. We have drawn close to the eternal truths of the Word of God that are found in doctrines that have been around forever, for you, for me, for all humanity. But our feet have barely touched the shore of an expansive and very deep sea. We have seen but a few twinkling stars in a vast universe. There is infinitely more out there. There is a door and a path on high inviting us to enter and to advance toward new and better lives.

Nobody is obliged to walk the path of others. All should make their own decisions—theirs alone. But one thing I know for certain: you and I need the watch care of a Father, He who says, "Behold, I stand at the door and knock; if any one hears my voice and opens the door, I will come in to him and eat with him, and he with me" (Revelation 3:20).

When you hear the Spirit inviting you to come and know God, do not turn Him away. That is where life is found. Give yourself to Him.

Soon these words will come true: "The great controversy is ended. Sin and sinners are no more. The entire universe is clean. One pulse of harmony and gladness beats through the vast creation. From Him who created all, flow life and light and gladness, throughout the realms of illimitable space. From the minutest atom to the greatest world, all things, animate and inanimate, in their unshadowed beauty and perfect joy, declare that God is love."[3]

FOR YOUR REFLECTION

1. When will the kingdom be given to Christ?

2. Who guarantees this promise?

3. What does it mean to *keep watch*?

4. What does the second coming of Christ mean to you?

1. Friedrich Nietzsche, *Human, All Too Human,* 102.

2. Antonio Machado, poem 6 from "Moral Proverbs and Folk Songs," in *Times Alone.*

3. Ellen G. White, *The Great Controversy Between Christ and Satan* (Mountainview, CA: Pacific Press®, 1950), 678.

Works Consulted

Adawiyya, Rabiʻa al-. "If I Adore You." Translation supplied by the author.

Alighieri, Dante. *Paradise*. In *The Divine Comedy*. Translated by A. S. Kline. 2000. http://www.poetryintranslation.com/PITBR/Italian/DantPar1to7.htm#anchor_Toc64099811.

Augustine, Saint. *The Confessions*. Translated by J. G. Pilkington. Vol. 1 of *Nicene and Post-Nicene Fathers,* edited by Philip Schaff. Buffalo, NY: Christian Literature Publishing, 1887. Revised and edited by Kevin Knight for New Advent. www.newadvent.org/fathers/110101.htm.

Baudelaire, Charles. "Destruction." Translation supplied by the author.

———. "To the Reader." In *Flowers of Evil,* translated by Jacques LeClercq. Mount Vernon, NY: Peter Pauper Press, 1958.

Campechano, Alfredo. "Bread."

———. "Temptation."

Dostoyevsky, Fyodor. *The Brothers Karamazov*. Translated by Richard Pevear and Larissa Volokhonsky. New York: Farrar, Straus and Giroux, 2002.

Eco, Umberto. *The Name of the Rose*. San Diego, CA: Harvest Books, 1994.

Eliot, George. *Romola*. Project Gutenberg, 2007. http://www.gutenberg.org/files/24020/24020-h/24020-h.htm.

Galeano, Eduardo. *El libro de los abrazos*. Buenos Aires: Siglo XXI Ed., 1989.

Halevi, Judah. "Lord, Where Shall I Find You?" Translation supplied by the author.

Henry, Matthew. *The Comprehensive Commentary on the Holy Bible: Acts-Revelation*. Edited by William Jenks. Brattleboro, VT: Brattleboro Typographic Co., 1839.

Jiménez, Juan Ramón. "Whatever You Want." Translation supplied by the author.

Kancyper, Luis. *Resentimiento y Remordimiento*. Buenos Aires: Paidós, 1991.

Kant, Immanuel. *Critique of Pure Reason*. Translated by J. M. D. Meiklejohn. Reprint of the 1855 London edition, Project Gutenberg, 2003. http://www.gutenberg.org/files/4280/4280-h/4280-h.htm.

Kelly, Thomas. "Zion Stands by Hills Surrounded." 1806.

Kierkegaard, Søren. *Søren Kierkegaard's Journals and Papers*. Vol. 5,

Autobiographical Part One, 1829–1848. Translated and edited by Howard
    V. Hong and Edna H. Hong. Bloomington, IN: Indiana University Press,
    1978.

Lazarus, Emma. "The New Colossus." 1883.

Lewis, C. S. *Mere Christianity.* New York: Macmillan, 1960.

Lugones, Leopoldo. *Lunario sentimental.* Buenos Aires: M. Gleizer, 1909.

Machado, Antonio. Poem 6 from "Moral Proverbs and Folks Songs." In *Times
    Alone: Selected Poems of Antonio Machado,* translated by Robert Bly. Middle-
    town, CT: Wesleyan University Press, 1983.

———. "The Search."

Neruda, Pablo. *Confieso que he vivido.* Barcelona: Seix Barral, 1974.

Nietzsche, Friedrich. *Human, All Too Human.* Translated by Alexander Harvey.
    Reprint of the 1908 Chicago edition, Project Gutenberg, 2011. https://
    www.gutenberg.org/files/38145/38145-h/38145-h.htm.

Ortega y Gasset, José. *Estudios sobre el amor.* Antología. 2ª edición. Madrid:
    Editorial Plenitud, 1963.

Pascal, Blaise. *Pensées.* Translated by W. F. Trotter. Reprint of the 1958 New
    York edition, Project Gutenberg, 2006. http://www.gutenberg.org
    /files/18269/18269-0.txt.

Shalamov, Varlam Tikhonovich. *Relatos de Kolimá.* Vol. 1. Barcelona: Editorial
    Minúscula, 2007.

White, Ellen G. *Christ's Object Lessons.* Washington, DC: Review and Herald®,
    1947.

———. *The Desire of Ages.* Mountain View, CA: Pacific Press®, 1940.

———. *God's Amazing Grace.* Hagerstown, MD: Review and Herald®, 2004.

———. *The Great Controversy Between Christ and Satan.* Mountain View, CA:
    Pacific Press®, 1950.

———. *Selected Messages.* Book 1. Washington, DC: Review and Herald®,
    1958–1980.

———. *Thoughts From the Mount of Blessing.* Mountain View, CA: Pacific
    Press®, 1956.